Toxic Goals, Flow
and the
Pursuit of Excellence

Overcoming Boredom & Fear on
Your Way to a Better Life

Charles MacInerney

Flaming Leaf Press

Cover design by: Charles MacInerney

Printed in the United States of America

Flaming Leaf Press

ISBN: 978-0-9973012-8-1

*To all those who seek to understand
and participate
in the evolution of consciousness.*

CONTENTS

vi

ANNOTATED CHAPTER OUTLINE

Introduction

Americans dedicate vast resources in the futile attempt to escape from their boredom and fear. The entertainment industry promises us relief from boredom; the insurance industry offers us relief from anxiety. If money could solve these problems, why do so many millionaires and billionaires suffer from these same issues? Drugs, legal and illegal, may allow us to escape for a time, but at what price and for how long? Fortunately, there is a simple solution to both boredom and anxiety that works, is available to everyone, and it's free.

Chapter 1: Flow

Recognizing the relationship between goals and skills is crucial. When goals are set too high for our skill level, we are anxious; when they are set too low, we are bored. It is easy to understand. In practice, however, it turns out to be quite challenging to control our goals. Unconscious goals drive most people. After a quick review and explanation of the work of Mihaly Csikszentmihalyi, we will expand on his model to show: the importance of breaking goals into smaller steps; how to employ fluid goal setting; that size does matter (when talking about the width of a person's "Flow window"); and how to expand that window, leading to more and deeper states of Flow.

Chapter 2: Toxic Goals

When confronted with a toxic goal, quitting is exactly the right response. Yet, there is a strong cultural bias against giving up. This chapter divides commonly held toxic goals into 16 categories, shows why they are toxic, and how you can recognize them. The ways to release a toxic goal (which are not always easy) will have to wait until Chapter four.

Chapter 3: Circle of Failure

Most people have a clear idea of how failure looks. Success is often vague, defined in terms of not failing. These "negative goals" are seldom chosen deliberately. They tend to lurk beneath the surface of awareness but are all the more potent for being somewhat invisible. The Circle of Failure is a model that illustrates this situation, helping the reader understand intuitively how toxic goals create boredom and fear and ultimately manifest the failure they seek to avoid.

Chapter 4: Blue Dot of Success

To break the cycle of boredom and fear, we must replace toxic goals with the appropriate positive goals. A new model that I call the "Blue Dot of Success" demonstrates this principle. Success is defined clearly in this model, and failure does not exist. This model helps us to identify goals that will manifest Flow, thus increasing the likelihood of success. It reveals the secret of releasing toxic goals. Finally, it illustrates why attaining a goal (even a positive goal) eventually leads to boredom and anxiety and shows us the secret to surviving our success.

Chapter 5: Living Your Flow

Goals seldom exist in isolation. They form complex groupings that interact with each other, for better or worse. Driving to work this morning, you might have had three goals, none of which you consciously chose when you climbed behind the wheel: get to work on time, get to work alive, and don't spill your Cinnamon Dolce

Chapter 6: Flow Is the Answer

We will look at various problems, including the healthcare system, education, the politicization of science, the war on drugs, the war on crime, and our fear of change. In each case, we will see how toxic goals can trap us in a Circle of Failure. As individuals and as a society, if we can erase these toxic goals and find our own Blue Dot of Success, there is no telling what we can achieve. That is the miracle of Flow! We will close this chapter by looking at how these principles hold up under the most challenging circumstances, like how we face the process of aging and our inevitable mortality.

Chapter 7: Closing Thoughts

We will conclude with a short invocation for how to live your life in Flow, cliff notes to help readers retain vital concepts, and remind them that these ideas are practical only if practiced. The book concludes with two inspirational quotations to tie it all together.

ILLUSTRATIONS

All graphs and illustrations in this book are printed in grey-scale.

If you would like to see the Full Color original illustrations please visit *ToxicGoals.com*.

INTRODUCTION

"A person who has mastered dharana (concentration), knows what they want, and society parts before them, like butter before a hot knife." ~ Yoga Aphorism

What is the secret to never being bored? Is it possible to master your fear? Are you capable of sustaining deep concentration in pursuit of your highest aspirations? For those who wish to live in Flow with the universe, this future is within reach. You are holding it in your hands.

The first step on this journey of self-actualization will be to master the use of goals. This includes knowing which goals to embrace and how to manifest them. But the real challenge lies in identifying and releasing toxic goals.

There are many categories of toxic goals that we will examine. These include goals that increase anxiety or lead to boredom and those that cause harm to ourselves, family, friends, or society. We will also look at goals imposed on us, those that we have outgrown, or that distract us from our vision. Most importantly, we will look at objectively toxic goals.

This book did not come easily. The concepts emerged over three decades, incomplete and tangled up with my personal story. It took time to identify, isolate, and assemble these ideas into a cohesive paradigm. It took practice to learn how to use these ideas to heal my past, live in the present, and reinvent my future. This book has grown out of a lifetime of challenges and mistakes and the desire to make sense of it all.

***

As a kid, I spent a lot of time dreaming about what I would do with my life. I held on tightly to those plans, even after they proved impossible, which led to disappointment and frustration.

Although both of my parents were 100% native Texans, I grew up in a small English village, eight miles from Oxford, called Bladon. I was a choir boy at the local church where Sir Winston Churchill was buried. We shared our village with tourists from around the world who came to pay their respects at his gravesite.

I celebrated my 11th birthday in 1972 during the worst year of the Northern Ireland Conflict. It started with the "Bloody Sunday" massacre in Derry – 14 dead and another 14 wounded by British soldiers. The IRA responded with 20 car bombs over 80 minutes, killing nine and injuring 130 people in London. Paul McCartney's song, "Give Ireland Back to the Irish," was banned by the BBC. The coal miners were on strike, and my father kept us occupied during the resulting blackouts by playing card games with us by candlelight. These were stressful times for us all. My mother and older sister were taking yoga classes and decided that I needed yoga as much as they did. This is how I met my first yoga teacher, Arlene Council. It was Arlene who taught me how to relax, breathe, and focus my attention. These skills led to my first experience of a peak experience, or what athletes often refer to as being in the zone or being in Flow.

As much as my mother loved Eastern philosophy, my father loved science. He taught physics and chemistry but also had degrees in philosophy, history, and sociology. Looking back, it seems inevitable that I would try to bridge the gap between these two most pervasive influences on my early life – Western science and Eastern philosophy. At its heart, yoga is the science of human consciousness. It is arguably the oldest such discipline still practiced in the world today. My interest in yoga psychology led me to pursue meditation, improve my mental focus, and ultimately write this book.

We spent ten wonderful years in Bladon, living in an old manor house called The Beeches. The front door was salvaged from the old Oxford castle and thought to be over 800 years old. The back yard included 11 acres of massive 200-year-old beech trees, apple orchards, and ornamental gardens. We looked out across a valley full of grazing cattle to see Blenheim Palace in the distance.

One of my sisters was dating an Oxford student. He was a regular guest at our house on weekends and holidays and often brought his friends to visit. In turn, they invited us to events on their campus. I fell in love with Oxford, both the town and the university. I set my sights on attending Oxford when I was old enough.

But when I was 14, my father announced that we would be moving to Ireland the following year, when he retired from teaching. We were so happy where we were that it had never occurred to me that we might someday leave. I knew little about Ireland. What I did know came from watching the BBC news reports of political upheaval and violence. I did not have many close friends and did not want to lose them. The idea of making new friends in Ireland was daunting, especially considering I had a thick English accent.

My two oldest siblings had long since moved out on their own. The third, who was 20, announced that she would be staying in England with her boyfriend. My parents did not give me a choice.

I spent the next summer in Ireland, camping with my parents in a sheep field where my father planned to build his dream home. We had no electricity, water, or plumbing. Neither did our neighbors who had lived on the peninsula for generations! The more I fixated on what I was leaving behind, the more miserable I became.

My parents grew frustrated by my sullen demeanor. Our nearest neighbors, the Roaches, had a son. Paul was my age, and my mother suggested that I make friends with him. The next day she volunteered me to help the Roaches on their farm.

There were only a few days of dry weather to get the cut hay off the ground, and the farm needed all the help they could get. From the road, I saw a small group gathering in the far corner of the field. They wasted no time in putting me to work. Mrs. Roach circled higher and higher on top of a growing haystack, catching the bundles of grass as we tossed them up to her with our three-pronged pitchforks, and carefully arranging the hay into a waterproof thatch. I was out of sync with everyone around me, always in the wrong place at the wrong time, and repeatedly told, "Mind yourself, Lad!"

At some point, I noticed that I was not thinking anymore! I was lost in the rhythm of the work and those around me. I understood and found my place in the intricate choreography of a family working together for common cause. For the next few days, I was too busy to think during the day and too tired to think at night. Although I did not have the language to describe it at the time, I was in Flow!

The next week, I helped milk the cows and then accompanied Mr. Roach when he delivered the milk on his horse-drawn cart to a nearby hotel. On the way home, we stopped at a pub, and he bought me a pint of shandy (a mixture of beer and fizzy lemonade). In the afternoon, I helped him in his forge. I stood in the shadows, working the cracked leather bellows, as he hammered out the glowing red iron against the anvil. He grinned from ear to ear, wiping the sweat from his brow as he worked. When I asked what we were making, he threw out his chest and announced it was a tool of his own design that he called a "digger." To me, it just looked like a blunt and twisted hand sickle. But the next morning, when I used it to help the Roaches dig for cockles on the mudflats at low tide, I had to admit, when asked, that the digger was indeed the perfect tool for the job.

The more I let go of my old dreams of England, the more room I had for new ones. I fell in love with the natural beauty of the land. Our small peninsula was surrounded on three sides by the waters of Dingle Bay. The bay was, in turn, framed on three sides by mountains. A dozen lakes glinted in the sunlight, and double and triple rainbows were a regular occurrence.

Some days I would climb down the cliff to our private beach. Other days, I would follow a fast-running trout stream into the mountains. I realized that I was happy and began to envision going to the local school for a couple of years, then moving to Dublin and enrolling at Trinity College, which my father pointed out was considered the equal of Oxford and Cambridge. Paul and I were becoming friends, and I grew confident that I could make a new life in Ireland.

Then my world turned inside-out once again. The local authorities rejected my father's application for planning permission to build his house. He was furious. "That's it!" he declared, "We are moving back to Texas, where, by God, a man's land is his own!"

The next year I found myself living in a barn on a hundred acres of undeveloped East Texas hardwood forest. Our neighbor on three sides was Temple Lumbar Inc., which owned a million acres of pine trees. Once again, we were camping with no electricity, plumbing, or running water. Once again, I was miserable. Coming from Ireland, everything in Texas looked brown, even the grass.

At some point, I concluded that dreams were a waste of time and a source of disappointment. Starting my junior year at my new high school, I had no desire to invest in planning for the future.

Because I lacked any direction, adults were more than happy to provide it for me. My math teacher pushed me to apply to SMU. My speech coach secured a scholarship for me at a small college with a strong theatre department. My physics teacher assumed I would study physics.

I ended up following a couple of friends who had enrolled at nearby Stephen F. Austin State University, which had a decent undergraduate physics department.

Regrettably, I had little emotional commitment to the goal of getting a degree in physics. This resulted in a half-hearted approach to my studies. By the end of my first semester at college, I was struggling with boredom. This was especially true when trying to study, which was most of the time. I was also struggling with loneliness due to increasing social anxiety. My desire to be liked by others morphed into a fear of being disliked. Most of the time, I was either anxious or bored.

I moved to Austin in the mid-1980s to study mathematics and computer science at the University of Texas. It was here that I first encountered the work of the renowned psychologist, Mihaly Csikszentmihalyi. His insight into the relationship between goals and skills was a revelation to me. I was especially interested in how some goals can result in boredom, and others lead to anxiety.

Since moving to America, I had suffered from fear, boredom, and regret. I finally knew why. I had forgotten how to choose my own goals. Instead, I had been trying to live up to other people's expectations. Most of my goals were unconscious and toxic. I determined to change.

My second revelation was that I had no interest in pursuing a degree. The only reason I was in school was to avoid disappointing my family, plus a fear that I could not make a good living without a college education. I knew pursuing a degree (that I did not want) played a large part in my current unhappiness. I also knew that the pursuit of a degree was distracting me from the most important question I needed to be asking: What do I want to do with my life? So, I dropped out of school midway through my senior year, despite having good grades.

It took some time, but eventually, I realized that I wanted to teach yoga. Since moving to the US, this was the first time that I committed to a goal that was genuinely mine. In the 1980s, yoga was considered a hobby, not a career. I did not care. I began using my newly-acquired, goal-setting skills to manifest my own dreams. Almost immediately, the boredom and anxiety fell away, and I began to experience more Flow in my life. Everything, including myself, came into focus. I felt like the universe was now supporting my aspirations rather than blocking them. As my confidence increased, new opportunities started to come my way.

In 1991, the University of Texas hired me to teach a three-hour workshop for their faculty and staff on yoga. The topic was improving concentration. They asked me to explore the subject from an Eastern perspective. The workshop was well-received, but I was personally disappointed. I was already utilizing the idea of Flow in my own life to good effect. However, when I shared these principles with the audience, my explanations felt convoluted, and the audience seemed somewhat confused.

I was surprised when the university invited me back to teach the same workshop again. I immediately began distilling and organizing my thoughts into a format that audiences could quickly grasp and implement. Over the next few years, I taught this workshop 45 times to UT faculty, staff, students, and athletes (women's track, golf, and volleyball teams). With each repetition, I found new ways to improve on the content and delivery. In 1994, a company called 3M (best known for inventing Post-It Notes) hired me to talk about goal setting to a group of engineers. I followed this presentation with workshops for Motorola, Sematech, IBM, Apple, dozens of smaller businesses, universities, government agencies, and various conferences.

Whether I was working in a corporate meeting room or with athletes in a gym, I noticed similar messages plastered on the breakroom walls: "It's always too early to quit."; "Cowards never start, and winners never quit."; "The moment you're about to quit is the moment right before the miracle happens. Don't give up." Curiously, these posters attributed almost all of the quotations to anonymous sources.

We have a cultural blind spot concerning goals. We praise those few individuals who cling to dreams regardless of the odds or the cost. We celebrate those few who end up succeeding while ignoring all of those who risk everything and fail.

On the other hand, those who give up a dream are met with, at best, embarrassed silence. Quitting is often seen as worse than failing! How many times have you heard someone say, "At least they tried!"?

From my teenage years, being moved from England to Ireland and then to Texas, I learned that even the best dreams could become toxic in the face of changing circumstances. Clinging to a toxic goal inevitably leads to disappointment and suffering. Sometimes letting go of a dream is not only the smart choice but the more difficult and courageous choice.

There are hundreds of books written on setting and achieving goals, but few on the art of quitting. At last search, I only found *The Dip: When to Stick and When to Quit* by Seth Godin. I enjoyed reading Godin's book, but it only dealt with one aspect of quitting and more closely resembled a blog post than a book.

Since 1992 I have led over 50 yoga retreats in Mexico, Guatemala, Costa Rica, and several hundred weekend retreats throughout the US. In 1999, I saw a growing need for quality yoga teacher-training programs. Together with Donna Belk and Ellen B. Smith, we launched the Texas Yoga Retreat and the Living Yoga Program, which now has over 400 graduates teaching yoga in 45 states and 15 countries. At the heart of all that I practice and teach is the concept of Flow.

***

Goals are universal, essential, and unavoidable. Even an amoeba has objectives like eating while not being eaten! These goals may be unconscious or take the form of ancient drives, instincts, and desires. But regardless of what we call them, they affect how the amoeba behaves and reacts to its environment. There is no way to escape goals. If you do not choose your goals with deliberation, you will accumulate goals carelessly.

At any given moment, you may have dozens of goals at play simultaneously. For instance: When taking your kids to the museum, you might want them to have fun, be safe, not break anything, and think that you are the best parent in the world. You might also be hoping to have a little downtime to relax with a cappuccino or spend more than 30 seconds at an exhibit without distraction. Besides, you might be hoping to leave before rush-hour traffic gets bad. You might wish for strangers to think you look far too young to be the parent of these children or that your spouse will notice and appreciate what you are doing. Some goals are small, some are petty, but all of them affect how you act and react as you move through the museum.

We do not choose whether or not to have goals. The real question is whether you are conscious of your goals. Are they chosen deliberately? Are the positive? Do they support your highest aspirations? And most importantly, do your goals serve you, or do you live in service to them?

Let's take a look at a goal that exerts a strong influence on most people. No matter how much or how little money they have, most people would like more, not less! If you include yourself in this category, try listing the reasons you want more money. Every single reason you come up with is probably an attempt to fend off either boredom or fear. So we could argue that money is merely a means to an end. What you want is less boredom, less fear, and more Flow in your life.

For those living in poverty, increased wealth may reduce anxiety and boredom, at least for a time. However, as with any drug, we can soon build up a tolerance to money. Distracting ourselves from boredom or fear becomes increasingly more expensive and less effective. This is especially true for the wealthy. The rich often struggle to escape from boredom because so little is required of them to survive. They also struggle more with anxiety, as they have so much more to lose.

Once you realize that more money is not the solution to escaping boredom and fear, you must look elsewhere for answers.

Boredom and fear are internal states of mind. External solutions will always miss the mark. This book will show you the most effective and proven ways to manage boredom and fear by choosing better goals. Goals can help you enjoy the present moment and shape your future to benefit yourself, your family, society, and the planet. When they fail to do this, they are toxic. This book will provide you with the tools you will need to notice, identify, and replace toxic goals with something better.

Not all Flow experiences are equal. Those that have experienced Deep Flow know that it is autotelic – a reward in and of itself. When asked to identify a favorite memory, most people will recall a moment in which they were focused entirely on something - whether it was seeing the Grand Canyon, a perfect golf swing, or holding their newborn baby for the first time. Those moments of perfect focused attention are moments of Flow, which infuse our lives with meaning.

If you believe in free will, in the idea that your fate is not predetermined, then the question becomes: What kind of a future do you wish for yourself? The skills outlined in this book may take time to master, but this is time well spent, as success will deliver a prize beyond the reach of even the wealthiest – a life of Flow, filled with magic, meaning, and purpose.

***

The first two chapters of this book introduce, expand and explore the concepts of Flow and Toxic Goals.

The third and fourth chapters compare negative goals (which most people have) with positive goals. They demonstrate why negative goals are self-sabotaging and lead to suffering and why using positive goals helps us escape this trap. They will also show you how to expand your Flow window so that you experience more and deeper Flow in your life.

The fifth chapter recognizes that goals do not exist in isolation but are embedded in a complex web of interconnected and interdependent goals, aspirations, and dreams. At this level, we must understand and organize our goals if we are to avoid getting trapped in a tangled web of competing intentions, objectives, and ambitions.

The sixth chapter starts with practical examples of how these principles can help us understand and solve a variety of problems that we encounter in our personal life and society. It closes with a discussion of Flow's spiritual implications and shows how the book's ideas can help us, both in life and how we approach our mortality.

The last chapter will close with a short review of the materials discussed, and suggestions for how to move forward.

***

This is what I wish for you, your family, friends, and the world: To live a life not spent reacting to primitive needs and unconscious drives but in passionate service to your highest aspirations.

Chapter One

FLOW

In 1964, Abraham Maslow began studying what he referred to as Peak Experiences. He described these as "rare, exciting, oceanic, deeply moving, exhilarating, elevating experiences that generate an advanced form of perceiving reality, and are even mystic and magical in their effect upon the experimenter." Maslow was by no means the first or last person to study the peak experience. With its roots dating back over three thousand years, yoga uses heightened states of concentration called dharana (the sixth limb of yoga) to facilitate deeply spiritual/mystical states of mind. Modern-day business gurus refer to peak performance, and athletes talk of "being in the zone."

During the 1980s, Mihaly Csikszentmihalyi, one of the world's leading researchers on positive psychology, studied and compiled research on autotelic experiences (actions performed for their own sake). He was fascinated by people who were able to achieve more profound levels of concentration. Csikszentmihalyi realized that athletes, Tibetan monks, and chess players described a similar pure, effortless concentration.

From observing a wide variety of people who excelled at concentration, he distilled a basic algorithm that anyone can use to improve their ability to focus their attention.

In 1990, Csikszentmihalyi published his groundbreaking book, "Flow: The Psychology of Optimal Experience." The term Flow, which I will use throughout this book, comes from his work.

Flow can occur in meditation, playing chess, or working on a math problem. It can be challenging for an observer to know the performer's state of mind unless you are an expert in the activity they are performing.

Imagine watching two people who are meditating. One is experiencing Deep Flow, and the other is wondering what he will have for dinner. Most of us would not be able to tell the difference. Thus, I will focus on Flow experiences that are physical and, therefore, easier to recognize and appreciate.

Flow in Sports

Magic Johnson is considered one of the best passers in the history of basketball. Watching him play, you begin to understand why Maslow used terms like "mystic" and "magical" to describe a peak experience.

One of the stand-out performances of the 1976 Summer Olympics in Montreal was Nadia Comaneci. Representing Romania, at the age of 14, Nadia was the first gymnast in the history of the Olympics ever to receive a perfect 10. Then she went on to do it six more times. As she flew through the air, spinning, twisting, and looking for the ground to nail her landing, do you think there was any part of her mind that was wondering about endorsements? Of course not. She was utterly focused, in the present moment, in Flow with the performance of her routine.

I heard two researchers talking about the neuroscience behind a baseball player attempting to hit a 98-mile-an-hour fastball. It takes 100 ms (one-tenth of a second) for the batter's eye to pick up the ball and the brain to process the image. Once the brain decides what to do, it takes 25 ms for the signal to reach the muscles to initiate the swing. It takes another 150 ms to complete the swing. That comes to 275 ms. Here is the problem: A 98-mph fastball reaches the plate in less than 400 ms. So, the batter's brain only has 125 ms, from when it first sees the ball, to decide whether or not to swing.

During this time, the brain has to begin tracking the ball's path, estimate the speed and trajectory of its flight, and calculate where and when the ball will cross the plate. It still has to decide if there is any spin on the ball, and if so, calculate the effects and adjust accordingly. Then whether or not to swing and when to initiate the swing must be determined. When you consider that most people take 350 ms to blink, 125 ms is not much time.

The two researchers declared that it is scientifically impossible to hit a 98-mph fastball. They followed up by saying that if they had not just seen a major-league baseball player do precisely that, they would stick to their story. In today's game, the fastest pitchers are pushing 105 mph. As Yogi Berra once said, "How can you hit and think at the same time?" The secret of doing the impossible is to find Flow, and spectators will pay large sums of money to witness athletes deliver on this promise.

When I was 11, I saw a demonstration of the Samurai horseback archery called Yabusame on TV. The archers, at full gallop, drew their bows and released their arrows. Every archer hit the center of the bull's-eye. I knew that this was impossible! My father taught physics and had explained it to me one day while watching a Western. The villain was shooting from the back of the train, which was lurching to-and-fro.

"Don't worry," my father said, "He can't hit anything," When I asked, he explained. "If you stand on solid ground and aim at a target, and the target moves six inches, the most that you will miss (if you are a marksman) is six inches.

On the other hand, if the target is held steady, but the shooter is bouncing around up to six inches, they could easily miss 50 feet."

I turned to my father and asked him how the archers, bouncing on the back of a horse, could hit the target. It was the first time my father did not have an answer for me. Instead, he lit his pipe and changed the subject.

I followed my mother into the kitchen and asked her the same question. How can the Japanese archers hit the target from the back of a galloping horse? She answered, "Because… at the moment they release the arrow, they, the arrow, and the target are one!" Yogis call this state dharana, concentration taken to its highest expression. I call this state Deep Flow. In Deep Flow, the miraculous is commonplace.

Real Life Flow

Take a moment to think about a favorite memory of yours. I would put it to you that this is neither a memory of being bored or scared, nor thinking about the past or the future, but rather a memory of concentrated present-moment Flow! Our most compelling Flow experiences often result from facing and overcoming boredom or fear to achieve a peak experience. Most of us have moments of Flow that we can revisit in memory:

- A sunset on a beautiful beach
- Reading a favorite book
- Watching a great movie
- A perfect golf swing
- Falling in love

What is your favorite hobby? It is most likely an activity that helps you find moments of Flow, concentrating intensely on what you are doing, and not bored or scared. Whether we are talking about work, dating, sports, or hobbies, you have been seeking Flow. The trouble is that most people do not know they are looking for Flow. Thus, they seldom attain it, and even then, only by accident. To be clear, avoiding boredom or fear is not the same thing as seeking Flow.

Boredom and Fear

There is a concept in yoga philosophy that, over time, a strong attraction (raga) for something can lead to a strong aversion (dvesa) for its opposite. I heard a women's rights activist from the 1970s lament that what began as a love of feminism had devolved into a hatred for the masculine. A friend who loves native species has grown to hate "invasive" species. Just seeing bamboo can make her angry.

Likewise, the universally-shared desire for more Flow in life can readily become an aversion to its opposite: boredom and anxiety.

Think of how much money we spend trying to escape our boredom or fear with little or no success. A billionaire seeking to escape monotony buys a new yacht. For a few days, he is excited, but then apathy inevitably returns. Seeking to escape anxiety, he hires bodyguards and installs a new security system. For a few days, he might feel safer. But soon, he is once again waking up in the middle of the night to a strange sound. Escaping boredom and fear can be a costly proposition, and at best, offer only temporary success.

When we blame our circumstances for boredom and fear, we are lost. There is no end to how much money we can spend and still find ourselves bored or scared. The idea that we can escape boredom and fear by manipulating our external environment is fundamentally flawed. The only real control we ever have is over our reaction to that environment. Once you see this, you will realize that it is a cheaper solution to boredom and fear. More importantly, it is a solution that works.

Is it simple? Yes. Is it easy? No. It takes time and effort to learn how to control your internal reaction to your external environment. But if you were willing to work 40 hours a week at a job you did not enjoy, in an attempt to make enough money to escape boredom and fear, then perhaps it might make sense to spend a small fraction of that effort towards mastering control of your inner domain.

Distractions from Flow

Ask a tennis player what their goal is. If they say it is to win, they are lying. If that were indeed their goal, they would win every time they played tennis. Winning is easy! You could play against a five-year-old child and likely win, but that would be boring. Likewise, you probably do not seek out an opponent who is so far beyond your skill level that you cannot hope to hold your own because that is frustrating or even scary.

Without realizing it, you have been choosing opponents who will challenge you without intimidating you because your real goal was never to win but to find Flow while playing tennis.

Once we understand that we are looking for Flow, it is a little easier to avoid getting distracted by superficial goals like winning. With this inner clarity concerning our goals, our chances of finding Flow increase dramatically. As a side effect of finding Flow, performance improves, and so does the likelihood of winning. The trick is not to let anything distract us from our goal of staying in Flow. Winning and losing are distractions. Keep your eye on the real goal, and you will manifest more Flow in your life.

There are varying levels of intensity in Flow experiences. Although few have experienced Maslow's mystical, magical Peak Experience, almost all of us have memories of milder Flow experiences, and these moments make the rest of our lives seem worthwhile.

Basic Principles of Flow

If you google Flow, you will find numerous variations on two primary models. The one shown here is more complicated. I have chosen an older, simpler model of Flow.

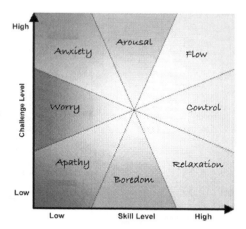

For the remainder of this book, we will use the model on the following page to explore the basic ideas of Csikszentmihalyi's work on Flow.

Then we will modify this simpler model to better illustrate pitfalls to finding Flow and solutions to living a life with more Flow.

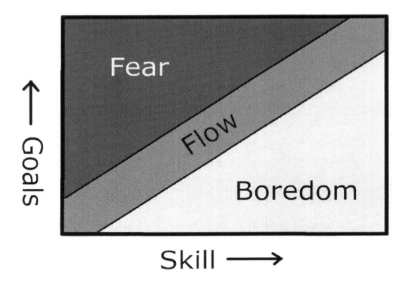

If you understand and practice using this model, you can reduce or even eliminate boredom and fear from your life.

Fear comes in many guises: unease, anxiety, angst, nervousness, worry, phobia, despair, dread, terror, panic, etc. It can also take the form of irritation, frustration, resentment, anger, or jealousy. Likewise, boredom has many flavors: apathy, ennui, lethargy, tedium, indifference, lassitude, etc. For simplicity's sake, I will usually use the words "fear" and "boredom" to refer to any similar state of mind.

In Csikszentmihalyi's Flow diagram, the vertical axis represents increasingly challenging goals or expectations. The horizontal axis represents increasing levels of skill.

When skills exceed goals, we are bored. When goals exceed skills, we are scared. When skills and goals are balanced, we will have more Flow in our lives and, correspondingly, less fear and less boredom.

Boredom and fear are ALWAYS a result of an imbalance between our goals and our skills. The implications of this are striking. If you can adjust this balance between goals and skills, you can find Flow.

Of the two variables, goals and skills, there is not much we can do in the here-and-now about our skill level. Over time, proficiency can certainly improve (or degrade). But in the present moment, you cannot change your level of skill. Goals, however, can be adjusted, raised, or lowered infinitely and instantly. So, if there is an imbalance between goals and skills, it makes more sense to change your plans.

If you are bored, identify the goal that is responsible for the boredom. Erase that goal, and then choose a new destination, raising the bar just high enough to restore Flow. If you are scared, again, identify and erase the goal causing the fear. Then choose a new purpose, lowering the bar just enough to restore Flow. It is simple! However, that does not mean that it is easy.

Learning to identify and control your goals is quite challenging. But to the degree you succeed, you will live a life beyond boredom and fear, living in the zone, delivering Peak Performances, and perhaps even experiencing on occasion what Maslow called the Peak Experience.

Overcoming Boredom

I taught my first yoga class in 1989. At first, I was a little nervous, but as my skill level improved, I found my Flow and fell in love with teaching yoga. I quit my tedious old job and immersed myself in the new role of a yoga teacher. Within three years, I was teaching 21 classes a week. Every lesson ended with the same pose, Shavasana. During this  deep-guided relaxation, I would lead students through the same progressive relaxation script. One day I realized that I was bored with teaching yoga. I could hear the boredom in my voice as I went through the progressive relaxation. I was pretty sure that my students could also tell that I was bored.

Rather than changing my environment (looking for a different career), I decided to look at how I reacted to my current situation. First, I examined my goal. When I first started teaching Shavasana, my goal was to make it through the entire script without forgetting anything or getting it out of sequence. This objective was suitable for a new and unskilled teacher. But after three years, teaching up to five classes a day, my skill level had increased, but not my goal! That was why I was bored!

First, I eliminated my old goal. I permitted myself to make mistakes with the script. Now that I was free from the previous goal, I could choose a new objective that would challenge my skill level and help me regain Flow. So, I started listening to the sound of my voice as I guided students through the relaxation.

I practiced resonating, relaxing my vocal cords, playing with how and when to stretch a word. Then I started playing with volume and pitch. Then I focused on the space between the words, listening to the silence, waiting for the perfect moment to pick up the next instruction.

I began to explore the acoustics of each room I taught in, bouncing my voice off walls, ceiling, and corners. I learned how to use the space to support my voice. As the students descended into relaxation, I noticed that I needed to soften the volume and deepen my voice pitch. I spaced out instructions with more and more silence, fading into the last meditative pause. I was no longer bored, and after 25 years of teaching, I still enjoy leading groups in guided relaxation and visualization. I play with my goals to stay in Flow, and I am never bored.

Overcoming Fear

As I gained a reputation in Austin as a yoga teacher, I started getting requests to talk about yoga, mind/body, stress management, improving concentration, and other related topics. A Houston-based company hired me to do a four-hour training course for them. They were coming to Austin for the day and asked me to teach a mind-mapping workshop in the morning. They were also paying me several thousand dollars, which was a lot more than I made teaching yoga! I entered the dates in my calendar and turned my mind toward more pressing matters.

Several weeks later, I woke up to hear my phone ringing. I listened to my answering machine pick up as I entered the shower. After dressing and feeding the dogs, I wandered into the office to check the message. It was from the Houston company. They were at the hotel in downtown Austin and wondering where I was. I checked my watch and saw that I was already ten minutes late. I called them back to apologized and offer them a full refund. They were not interested in canceling my workshop and asked me how long it would take to show up. "Twenty-five minutes," I replied.

Fighting down nausea, I grabbed a box and dumped in paper, pencils, and coloring pencils for 30 people, along with several books I might need. I threw on my best slacks and dress shirt and threw the rest of my clothes on the passenger seat. I put on socks at the first red light and shoes at the next.

Driving on Loop 1, I started to shave. Then I realized that I did not have the address or remember the name of the hotel. This was before the invention of cell phones, so I only had two choices. I could turn back and retrieve the address from my home computer, guaranteeing I would be much later than I promised, or drive on and hope I could remember the event's location in time.

Although I could not remember the hotel's name or address, I did have a vague feeling that it was near the river, east of Congress Avenue. I decided to gamble on recognizing the hotel when I saw it and drove on. Then I realized that I had exited the loop by habit, four exits early. Now I had to drive down Lamar Boulevard during morning rush hour. At one of the busier intersections, I waited for three complete rotations of the traffic light. I was gripping the steering wheel and rocking back and forth, trying to will the traffic light into turning green.

Then I realized that I was not in Flow. I was suffering from high levels of anxiety. If I showed up to lead a workshop in this state of mind, it would not turn out well. I realized that the red light was an opportunity for me to practice what I taught. I examined my goals. I wanted to give this organization a fantastic workshop, worthy of the money they were paying me, and I was hoping that this would lead to bigger and better offers in the future.

As I was already 20 minutes late, unorganized, and off my game, I realized that I was setting my goals way too high, resulting in anxiety and panic! So, I let go of the plan to wow the audience. I chose a new goal, more suited to where I found myself: That no matter how painful and embarrassing this situation might be, I would stay fully present to make sure I learned from this experience.

A calm resignation replaced the panic, and my mind cleared. I found the hotel right where I thought it would be. I was 45 minutes late.

A company representative escorted me to the podium but did not introduce me. As I started to introduce myself, one-third of the audience got up and walked out in protest. Usually, this would have rattled me, and things might quickly have gone downhill from there. Instead, I reminded myself of my new goal. No matter how painful it gets, I will stay present and learn from this experience.

I looked around at the audience members who had not walked out, smiled, and thanked them for staying. Then I started my program. It took some time, but I moved past any lingering embarrassment and found my Flow. I still had three hours to work with and an audience who seemed eager to learn.

Mastering Flow

People are pretty good at setting up initial conditions for finding Flow. Given a choice between two otherwise equivalent jobs, they will invariably choose the job less likely to be boring or scary. On their first day at work, their skill level is low. If the resulting anxiety is too great, they freeze up, and skill level remains stagnant. After a few days of suffering, they either quit, or their boss fires them. If, instead, they are only a little nervous on their first day, they will see a slight improvement in their skills.

For example, they might memorize their co-worker's names and learn the layout of the building. As their skills improve slightly, they have less anxiety, allowing them to concentrate more deeply and learn more quickly. As skills continue to improve, anxiety diminishes, and they find their Flow. This period may last a few days or weeks, or even longer. But as skills continue to improve, they find themselves slipping into boredom. At first, they may still perform well, despite being a little bored. However, it becomes increasingly likely that they will get so bored, and becomes a problem over time. They may grow to hate their work or start making careless mistakes.

You can see this pattern represented in the adjacent Flow Diagram. As skills improve, Flow replaces anxiety, and eventually, boredom replaces Flow. At this point, the potential for unforced errors increases.

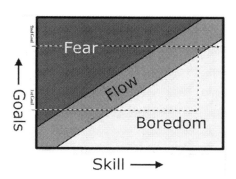

Weeks, months, and even years can pass unnoticed in this state of boredom before we notice and choose a new, more challenging goal.

What separates us from them? Us being those of us who live with boredom and anxiety and little, if any, Flow. Them being the Flow elite.

It turns out that the difference is in the number and spacing of the small steps (goals) along the path, leading from where they are to where they are going (their larger goal). Having more steps means smaller jumps and more control.

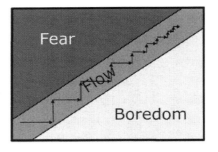

In the model below, with only two goals (arrows on the left of the chart), we have limited control over our Flow. If your skill level is in the middle of the horizontal axis, the easier goal is boring, and the more challenging goal is scary.

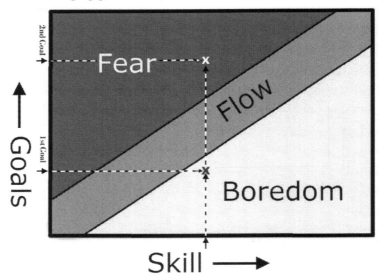

When you're bored or scared, learning shuts down, skills remain stagnant, and you are stuck. If you drop down to the lower goal, you are bored. If you jump up to the higher goal, you are scared. Eventually, you tire of being bored and scared. Unable to find Flow, you quit.

Compare the previous model to the one that follows. With more goals to choose from on the vertical axis, you can find one or more goals to put you in Flow, no matter your skill level. If you are in Flow, skill levels improve. As skill levels improve, you get bored and need to choose a new challenge to stay in Flow.

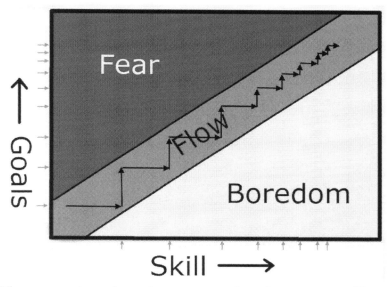

The more goals you have, the more control you have over your Flow. Notice that for any specific level of skill you can find one ore more three goals that can maintain Flow.

The deeper the Flow, the faster you improve. The faster your skills advance, the more frequently you must adjust your plans to stay in Flow. If you ever find your skill level has plateaued, look to your goals.

If your old goal has become monotonous, and the new goal is frustrating (fear), you will be stuck and unable to progress. The solution is to create a path from the easy goal to the challenging goal with at least one intermediary step. Between boredom and fear, you will always find Flow. But to find Flow, you may need smaller steps.

What separates us from them (the best performers in the world)? We might suffer through months or years of boredom or anxiety in a situation before recognizing the problem and taking steps to restore Flow. The best performers don't wait to restore Flow. They are continually recalibrating to stay in Flow.

Imagine two of the top tennis players in the world, Center Court at Wimbledon. If either player gets bored or anxious, they are more likely to make mistakes. How long do they have to recognize that they are not in the zone, identify and replace the responsible goal, and find their way back to Flow? At that level of play, a single mistake can make the difference between winning and losing. The best competitors in the world stay in Flow, even in challenging situations.

Imagine a free solo ascent of a rock face. There is no margin for error. That first mistake could easily be the last. If the climbers get bored or scared, they are more likely to make mistakes. If they lose their Flow, they cannot afford to go six months, or even six minutes, without noticing that they are not in Flow. The best rock climbers in the world stay in Flow. They do not get bored or scared while climbing, and if they do, they immediately notice and take corrective action to regain their Flow. That is why they are the best. Why do they climb mountains? Because that is where they find their Flow. The desire for Flow is such that many will risk their lives in pursuit of it.

Performance vs. Learning

Previously I stated that everyone is searching for Flow, often without realizing it. We also looked at how to control our goals to help find Flow. I may have given the impression that we should always seek Flow. But such a one-sided approach eventually leads to a shrinking cul-de-sac and does not end well.

There are two approaches to any activity: performing or learning. Performing is about finding Flow to achieve a flawless, perhaps even inspirational, performance. Learning is about pushing outside of your comfort zone to expand your abilities and improve your skills. It is about making and learning from your mistakes. Each requires a different strategy, and, like oil and water, they do not mix well. Always be clear about which you are engaged in, performing or learning, and set your goals accordingly.

There are times in life when it is essential to perform well. A conference once paid me an exorbitant fee to teach a single yoga class at their annual convention. I designed the program specifically for their attendees, used only my best tried-and-true material, prepared handouts, and made sure that I was already in Deep Flow when I started to teach. I did everything I could to make sure the class was a success.

A few weeks later, I taught yoga at a children's shelter. They could not afford an honorarium, but it was no less important to perform well and not make any mistakes. Other times, I seek out Flow purely for my own satisfaction.

When performance is not so critical, it can be an opportunity to learn and grow. In a learning environment, you push outside your comfort zone, make mistakes, and learn from those mistakes. An Austin high school once asked me to teach a yoga philosophy class to sophomores. The school ranked in the bottom 5% of schools in Texas. It was notorious for disciplinary problems, and 10th grade was the epicenter. Although they could not pay me, I saw this as an opportunity for personal growth and one more step in overcoming my anxiety with children. My intention with this class was to try out new material and approaches. I gave myself permission to make mistakes and learn from them.

After a rough start, I abandoned my original material, which was not working, and we turned the corner, ending on a high note. Mistakes were made, but I learned a lot from this experience. Moreover, the students participated, understood, and wanted to follow up with yoga independently. Having survived a day with 10th graders, I found myself more confident and better prepared to work with kids going forward, including at-risk youth.

Children tend to gravitate toward learning, adults toward performing. When exposed to a computer for the first time, a six-year-old can't wait to start playing with the mouse and keyboard. They make lots of mistakes, and they do not care because they learn how to use a computer.

Put a 70-year-old who has never used a computer in front of the same keyboard, and she hesitates. She does not want to touch a key because she is in performance mode, and does not want to make a mistake, so she does nothing and learns nothing.

This tendency for adults to be stuck in performance mode may have worked in the 12th century. After all, by the time you were an adult, you probably had already learned everything you needed to know. What the village expected from you was performance, not mistakes. But in the 21st century, everything is continually changing. The moment you stop learning, you start falling behind, whether you are 10 or 100.

The key to thriving in the changing world we find ourselves in is to seek learning opportunities whenever possible. But as adults, this goes against our natural inclinations. Twenty-first-century adults are still called upon to perform, to execute without mistakes. But we are also called upon to learn new things.

To succeed, we must cultivate the ability to switch our goals back and forth from performance to learning. This ability may not come naturally, but there is no reason that we cannot acquire it.

Dr. Don Wukash, a frequent participant in my Yoga & Creative Writing retreats, is a great example. He retired from a successful career as a heart surgeon - where performance was everything and mistakes unacceptable – to take up poetry. A few years later, despite being in his 70's, Don enrolled in a seven-year program to become a Jungian therapist.

As adults, we should be on the lookout for situations and environments where it is permissible to play, experiment, stretch our abilities, and make mistakes.

The first step in learning is to get outside your comfort zone. Deliberately put yourself in an environment where you do not know what to do (if you know what to do, you are not in a learning environment). Then do something, anything! The universe will give you feedback, positive and negative. If you pay attention to the feedback and link it to what you were doing, you can learn. As skills improve, you will get comfortable. Comfort is a signal that it is time to take another small step forward, balanced between the known and the unknown, where learning occurs.

Now, let's take a look at performance versus learning in relationship to our Flow model.

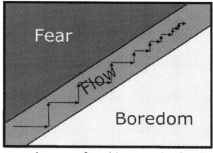

When you are in performance mode, your primary goal is to perform well. That means not getting bored or anxious in order to minimize any chance of making a mistake. In performance mode, you choose the goals that maximize your Flow.

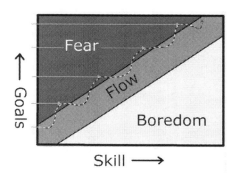

By contrast, in learning environments we raise our goals higher. Then we explore the space between Flow and anxiety. To do this, you must be willing to make mistakes. In this environment, learning has to be more important than performing.

When you look at learning in terms of Flow, you will see a similar phenomenon. People tend to stay in their comfort zone. Occasionally, they launch themselves too far into the unknown before quickly retreating to the safety of the status quo. At either extreme, boredom or anxiety, learning is not possible.

In a healthy learning environment, we try to stay right in the zone between knowing and not knowing. The more time we spend in this zone, the more rapidly we improve.

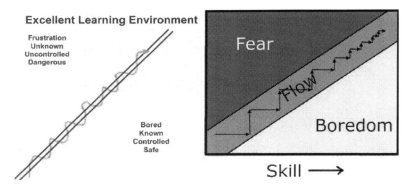

Expanding Your Window of Flow

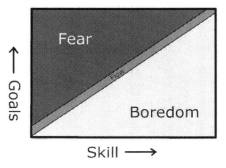

The Flow diagrams we have looked at so far are not representative of most people's ability to focus. A typical Flow window is much narrower.

Note that as the Flow window narrows, it becomes more challenging to find Flow.

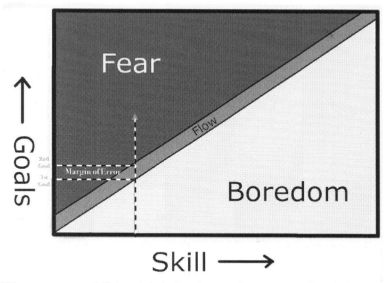

Whatever your skill level, it is harder to choose a goal to help you enter a Flow state. A goal that is slightly too-high will lead to anxiety. If it is too low it will result in boredom.

So naturally, the question arises: "How do you expand your Flow window?" If we reframe the problem, the answer might be easier to see. Instead of asking how to expand Flow, ask yourself, "How do I increase my tolerance of fear?" If you are scared of public speaking, how do you get over that fear? Now the answer is obvious: Face Your Fear!

In performance mode, we choose goals to put us in the zone. In learning mode, we seek out situations and select goals that will take us outside our comfort zone. If we continue to face our fears, eventually, we will increase our tolerance for anxiety. When you play at the edge of your ability, be prepared to make mistakes, but redeem those mistakes by making sure that you learn from them. Be careful!

If you confront your fear, but you are the first to blink, the fear gains power. You get weaker, and your Flow window shrinks further.

In *The Art of War*, Sun Tzu counsels us always to choose the time and place of battle to maximize our chance for victory. If you do not choose when and where to fight, your enemy will choose for you! If you avoid fear, you grow weaker, and the fear grows stronger. The further you retreat, the more fear advances. Eventually, you might even become a shut-in, ordering groceries to be delivered, afraid to leave your apartment. Sooner or later, you will still end up facing fear. There is no escape! If you do not choose the time and place of battle, fear will choose it for you. At 3 a.m., you will hear fear scrabbling at your bedroom door as you lie in the dark.

"Do the thing you fear to do and keep on doing it... that is the quickest and surest way ever yet discovered to conquer fear." ~ Dale Carnegie

Do not wait for fear to find you. Take control of the situation. You pick the time and place to face your fear! Then do not back down and make sure you win. If you are scared of public speaking and avoid it, you might one day find yourself being pushed out in front of an audience by your boss. In this situation, you might understandably descend into a primitive fight/flight/freeze response, letting down your boss. Such experiences can damage our self-esteem and result in increased anxiety.

Do not wait for fate to choose the time or place of a battle. Instead, maybe you could enlist the support of your children? Explain that you need their help to overcome your fear of public speaking. Ask them to be your audience. Then go to the bathroom and throw up. When you are ready, face your fear and overcome it. Deliver your talk across the

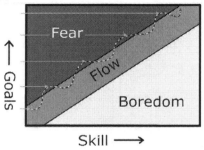

kitchen table to your kids. Remember, you must win this battle. If you fail, you will be weaker, and your fear stronger. So make sure you succeed.

As your skills improve, take baby steps. Choose each new goal in such a way that you know you can win the next battle. Invite a couple of friends to be your audience. Then join Toastmasters. With each success, you grow stronger and more confident. Keep pushing back on fear with small, deliberate steps. As you practice this in other areas of your life, you will build a greater tolerance for fear.

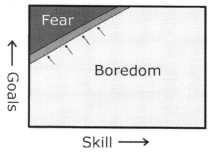

The problem is that this does not expand the Flow window; it just shifts the window upward! As your anxiety recedes, boredom takes its place.

On the other hand, if you set out to increase your tolerance for boredom, you can push down on the Flow window. Choose a monotonous activity and see if you can focus with one-pointed attention. When you succeed, you will discover the process is no longer tedious.

Boredom is not inherent in the activity. It is your inability or unwillingness to concentrate that results in boredom. Meditation is a beautiful example of this practice. Choose a target for your attention that would usually be boring, and then learn how to focus your mind on that target with one-pointed attention.

Just as with fear, choose the time and place for battle. Pick an exercise that you can win, and then be

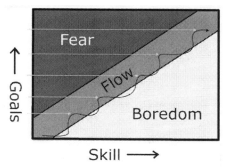

sure and win it. For instance, you can set your goal to focus with one-pointed attention on washing dishes for ten minutes. Pay as much attention to this process as you would if you were washing a newborn baby's face, or as a neurosurgeon aspires to, during surgery. Pick your goal and then nail it. Then choose another, more challenging goal as your meditative skills improve.

You can choose to focus on your breath, a mantra (sound), a yantra (geometric pattern), a prayer, or sit quietly and focus intently on nothing! If you can focus on nothing, you can focus on anything! When you discover that nothing is interesting, you will realize that nothing is boring anymore. As you practice this in all areas of your life, you will build a greater tolerance for boredom.

The problem is that this does not expand the Flow window either; it just shifts downward! As your boredom recedes, anxiety will take its place.

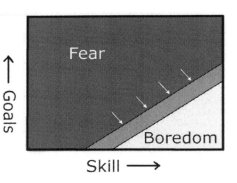

As you may already have guessed, you must push in both directions to open the Flow window. Regularly, choose something scary and learn how to control your goals and improve your skills until it is no longer scary. Then turn around and take on something boring, learn to control your goals, and find Flow in the most boring environment. If you push up against fear and push down against boredom, your Flow window will begin to open.

Why do so many of us have contracted Flow windows? Because rather than seeking Flow, which is a positive goal, most of us try to avoid boredom and fear. This is a negative goal. If we wanted more Flow in our lives, we would push in both directions, learning to overcome boredom and anxiety, resulting in an expanded Flow window.

If, on the other hand, we are trying to avoid either boredom or anxiety, we will actively avoid them. In so doing, the Flow window will shrink. Almost everyone has a bias or preference for either boredom or fear. We will consistently choose one over the other.

Some people hate boredom so much that given a choice, they will always choose anxiety. Others hate anxiety so much that they always push into boredom to avoid fear.

Here is the worst part of this predicament. The person who hates boredom so much that they always choose to face their fear (we call them 'adrenaline junkies') end up living lives of boredom. For a few hours on the weekend, they are in Flow, climbing El Capitan, or leaping out of a plane. But Monday morning, you find them dragging themselves back to work, facing five days of boredom, living only for the next weekend, and the opportunity to once again experience Flow.

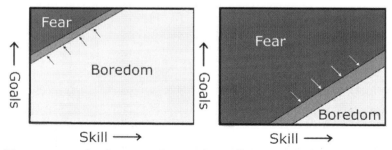

The person who hates anxiety ends up living a life full of fear. A cloistered monk fully absorbed with washing the dishes might feel trepidation at the prospect of leaving the monastery.

Few people choose to push in both directions. If you can maintain one-pointed attention for thirty minutes while washing dishes and not be bored, then fearlessly leap out of an airplane, your whole life opens up to Flow.

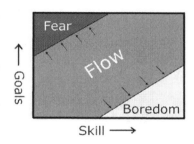

Remember, when it is crucial to perform well, set your goals to put yourself in Flow. When it is safe to make mistakes, expand your Flow window by facing down boredom and fear.

Deep Flow

There are two reasons for wanting to expand your Flow window. The first is to escape from boredom and fear. This is a toxic goal. It is fatally flawed as it requires deliberately experiencing the very thing you are trying to avoid. The alternative is to choose the positive goal of seeking more prolonged and profound Flow experiences. To do this, you have to get stronger mentally, so just as you might lift weights to build physical strength, you push into boredom and anxiety to build mental strength.

As your Flow window widens, three benefits become apparent: 1) You spend less time feeling bored or scared; 2) Whatever your skill level, it is easier to choose a goal that will put you in Flow; 3) Most significantly, you gain access to deeper states of Flow.

Csikszentmihalyi uses one term, Flow, to refer to all Flow states. I prefer to distinguish between mild Flow and what I call Deep Flow. Mild Flow is familiar to most people. It is a state where you are focused and performing well. You are in the moment, mind steady and not going off in a million directions. There is an absence of anxiety and boredom. This state is not even close to Deep Flow experiences.

In yoga, we call Deep Flow "dharana." This yogic state of focused attention is so complete that all sense of separation between you and your target merge into one unified state. In this merger, there is a loss of self or, to be more accurate, an expansion of self to include the other. All effort falls away; all thinking falls away.

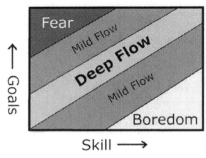

38

Time becomes malleable, contracting or expanding to help you accomplish your task.

Occasionally, time almost stops as you process vast amounts of information and act on it (like in a traffic accident). Other times it Flows effortlessly, like when you lose yourself in an outstanding performance. Some events feel as though time speeds up and slows down simultaneously.

One of my students, a retired major league baseball player, shared one of his own Deep Flow experiences. "The ball seemed to float over the home plate; I swear I could see the seams. I had all the time in the world." He was talking about hitting a home run off a 95-mph fastball. I asked him if he had ever struck out. He chuckled, "You can't even see that ball; it's coming at you that fast."

It is difficult for many who have experienced a Deep Flow moment to describe it. Words like "I" can ring false. A musician once talked about an out-of-body experience during a piano recital: "I did not play the piano... it was more like the music was playing through me.... I was standing to one side as a witness. When it finished, I felt like a fraud bowing and receiving applause for something that 'I' did not do."

Warning: Deep Flow is addictive! Once you have experienced Deep Flow, you will inevitably want more. The tragedy is when people first encounter a Deep Flow experience, they fall in love with the activity they were performing at the time. One person has a Deep Flow experience playing golf and thinks they love golf. Another thinks they love rock climbing. But what they love is the one-pointed state of mind they experienced while playing golf or climbing the mountain.

We surrender control only to find ourselves in Flow with the miraculous. Most mountain climbers, maybe all, are addicted to Flow. Why else would they leave behind their family and travel halfway around the world to climb a mountain like K2? As their skills improve, they get bored with the easier climbs and need more challenge to restore them to Flow. 'Adrenaline junkies' are notorious for their inability to deal with boredom.

I first experienced Deep Flow playing racquetball in college. After tearing up my knee in a wrestling tournament, I continued competing in racquetball tournaments, despite my doctor's repeated warnings. I reinjured my knee a dozen times over the next four years. Each time I would go back to crutches, then progress to a cane. Soon after, I would return to the racquetball court, promising myself, my friends, and my family to be more careful.

By the time I was ready to quit the sport, I had already destroyed the cartilage in both knees. Why did I refuse to follow my doctor's repeated requests to quit? Because I was not ready to give up Flow! The racquetball court was the only place where I escaped from boredom and fear and occasionally experienced magic.

After racquetball, I had to give up soccer, tennis, running, and eventually table tennis, bowling, and anything else that involved using my knees. I was 23 years old, and yoga was the only physical exercise that I could still manage. After giving up looking for Flow in competitive sports, I rediscovered it in my yoga practice. I finally realized that it was never Racquetball that I loved. It was a state of mind. I knew that I could find Flow in any activity once I learned to adjust my goals.

I have experienced Deep Flow while presenting at a medical conference, eating a tangerine during a thunderstorm, a near-miss experience on the freeway, boulder scrambling on the cliffs of Anglesey Island playing board games with friends. I no longer search for Flow in a particular activity. Any experience is an opportunity to find Deep Flow.

Most Deep Flow experiences last a few minutes or hours. But the after-effects can linger for days or weeks and fade slowly, like the sound of a great bell once struck. For days after a Deep Flow experience, traffic lights turn green as you approach, strangers smile, animals are attracted to you, and, as Joseph Campbell was fond of saying, "Doors open where before there were no doors." During this afterglow period, it feels like you can do anything you set your mind to, and without effort. The Deep Flow you find on a round of golf in the morning can translate into a higher math score in the afternoon.

There are two measures of a Flow experience; depth and breadth. A Deep Flow experience may be brief (it is hard to say as time is meaningless in this state), but this experience of oneness can lead to profound and lasting changes in anyone lucky enough to experience it. On the other hand, some Flow experiences may not be as profound but may last for days, weeks, or longer.

To be the best tennis player in the world, you must develop an expanded Flow window. During the countless hours of repetitive drills, often by yourself on the court mastering a specific skill, the enemy is boredom. The great players can practice day after day and be in Flow – as if what they are doing at that very moment was essential.

During a tournament, the enemy is fear. The great players can stay in Flow under severe pressure with the world's eyes watching and waiting for them to crack. If you excel at anything, chances are you already have a wide Flow window, at least when it comes to that particular activity.

The problem is that your relationship to Flow on the tennis court, the golf course, or doing a client's tax return does not necessarily translate into other areas of your life. A golfer may find Flow on the golf course, but not at home or work.

The trick is to realize it was not the golf you loved but the Flow you found on the golf course. When you understand this, you will begin to look for Flow, not just at golf but at home, at work, with your family and friends, when traveling, or napping in a hammock.

What separates "us" from "them" (the Flow Elite)? While we are just passing through Flow on our way from anxiety to boredom.

They are able to stay in Deep Flow more often and for extended periods of time.

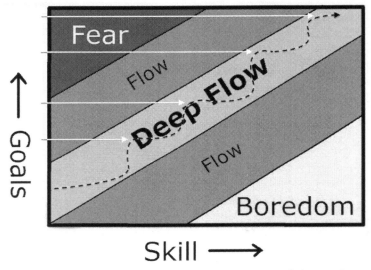

In closing, I would like to share part of a longer email from a former student (with her permission), which perfectly illustrates the ideas discussed in this chapter:

> ... On another note altogether, there is something far more important to me that I wanted to thank you for. I have been riding event horses more or less professionally since I was 16. It can be quite dangerous but I have never had any nerves at all, which was one of the main reasons that I was successful; I didn't get nervous and choke when a lot of other people did.
>
> Then, two years ago I had a really horrific crash, and I have been scared to get on a horse ever since then. I continued to ride because it was my life and my identity, and without the horses I felt like I had nothing, but I was miserable. I went to Australia in large part because I hoped a change of scene would provide a clean slate. I've spent the

past six months trying to decide whether to continue riding, dreading every day, or to quit and lose the life and lifestyle that I love.

To make a long story short, I was still undecided when I arrived at the intensive, though beginning to sway towards leaving the horse world behind. Your talks to us about Flow and about how our goals and skills relate and how fear and boredom affect our performance hit me like a ton of bricks. It was such a relief to finally accept the fact that I don't have to go out and be the best - to be perfect - every time I get on a horse.

The first time I rode again after the intensive, instead of concentrating on jumping five feet and looking beautiful and being perfect, I worked on jumping three feet, getting from one side to the other, preferably not falling off and having fun. And it worked! I was laughing and being silly and had fun on a horse for the first time in years.

The last few weeks have just gotten better and better. I can already nearly ride again at the level that I did a few years ago, and last night I accepted a job offer to go back to riding full-time, in the big league, after I finish school in December.

I don't think that I would have ever realized that sometimes it is okay to lower the standards and just accept where you are, at the moment, if it hadn't been for the intensive. I am literally happier than I have been in years. Thank you so much for your help; it has meant the world to me. Namaste. - Julie

Chapter Two

TOXIC GOALS

"Every man is wise when pursued by a mad dog, fewer when pursued by a mad woman; only the wisest survive when attacked by a mad notion."

~ Robertson Davies, Marchbanks

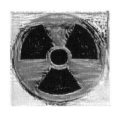

The Bias Against Quitting

Not all goals are healthy. No one questions that ambition can be compelling but that power can manifest evil as easily as good. Most of the literature on goals offers an abundance of advice on how to manifest your dreams. But what if your dream turns into a nightmare?

There is a strong cultural bias against quitting, especially in the USA. We celebrate heroes who, against all the odds, persevere through adversity to enjoy success and glory. Imagine a scenario where 100 participants compete for one large lottery prize. The more tickets they purchase, the more likely they are to be the winner. One player quits.

The other 99 risk everything. They sell their homes, cars, close out their savings accounts, and use every penny to finance their gamble. One wins the prize, and the remaining 98 contestants lose everything. Guess who is held up by the media as a hero? No, not the smart one who recognized the nature of the game and walked away! Not the 98 who failed. No, of course not. Everyone is talking about the courage of the one who put every last penny into the competition and won.

We hear a thousand variations of this story with the same theme: that perseverance is good, quitting is bad. And it is not just the news. The message is embedded in sports, literature, politics, etc. until we do not even question the statement anymore. There are times when quitting is the smart choice. A good poker player knows when to walk away from even the wealthiest pot. It is the rookie, unable to stop, who throws good money after bad.

When someone has a passionate dream and quits on it, friends and relatives often assume this is a failure. A 16-year-old girl who has wanted to be an astronaut since she could walk gives up on that dream. Maybe she quit out of fear. Perhaps she gave up due to laziness. Perhaps she recognized that she wants to be a mother more than an astronaut. Or it may be that she realized her real passion was for adventure and travel, which she could accomplish more effectively by working for an NGO in Sudan. Sometimes quitting is the smarter or more courageous choice, in which case, why not praise her for her decision?

I am not saying "never commit everything to the pursuit of a dream." I am merely advocating for a more balanced analysis of the situation. There are times when burning your bridge is the right choice. But sometimes the smart play is to walk away from the table and live to play another day.

Acquired Toxicity

Some goals are okay initially but become toxic over time. This is one of the most common problems that I see. A gymnast might dream of going to the Olympics. This goal might have been appropriate when she was ten years old. However, after rupturing the ACL in her knee, her doctor insists that she give up the sport. Now her goal of being in the Olympics can quickly become toxic. She might return to competition against her doctor's advice and suffer a catastrophic failure of the joint. Or she might continue to compete but hold back out of fear of re-injury, no longer excelling or even enjoying the sport. She might heed her doctor's advice and give up gymnastics, but hold onto the dream of gymnastics and slip into depression.

If this gymnast can shake herself free from the toxic goal of competing at the Olympics, an infinite variety of new options is open to her. Perhaps she could take up coaching other gymnasts. Alternatively, she could take up rock climbing, acting, or almost anything else that does not involve flying through space and landing hard.

Degrees of Toxicity

When you consider committing yourself to a new goal, take a moment to contemplate any possible toxic side effects. Examine the costs and benefits to your personal life and the complex web of your inter-relationships. Look at the costs and benefits in the immediate future and the distant future. Examine what this goal, if pursued, will cost you personally. Then expand outward to ask what it might cost your loved ones, your circle of friends, your country, the planet. Balance this against what you hope to gain. To the degree that the collective harm outweighs the collective benefits, this is a toxic goal, even if you stand to benefit in the short term.

Imagine you play for a high school basketball team, and you want to get a full scholarship to university. You hear that some scouts will be attending your next game. You decide that you want to do whatever it takes to get yourself noticed by the scouts. This goal has the potential to become toxic. Most of you reading this book would instantly recognize this possibility and without much effort. What would be the likely result of such a strategy?

In an attempt to stand out, you hog the ball, fail to pass, force difficult shots, and try to dribble your way out of every difficulty. Sure enough, you handle the ball more than your teammates. And yes, you do get the scouts' attention, but at what cost?

Worst case scenario: Your team loses because you are not playing as a team, and your teammates, your coach, and the scouts blame you for the loss. But even if you win, your actions may damage your relationship with the team. Next week and the week after that, you still have to play with them. You are part of the team, and you will be judged as much for the team's performance as for your own.

Your relationship with the whole is easy to see on a basketball team. It is harder to see it in the workplace with hundreds of employees. It is almost invisible at the level of a city, state, nation, or planet. But regardless of scale, and whether you can see it or not, you are always part of a greater whole. And the same principles apply at all scales. It is just that the consequences are less evident at the larger scales.

But do not fool yourself. There are always consequences, even if they seem remote and small. Throw a plastic bag on the ground and walk away. If no one sees you litter, what difference does it make in your life? But if six billion people are throwing plastic bags on the ground and walking away, you share in the collective guilt for the outcome. Each action you take, good or bad, changes who you are and how you feel. In the end, you are the one who must live with this evolving self.

There are different levels of toxicity among goals. But even the least toxic of goals is still destructive and must not be underestimated. Consider the issue of trust between partners. How much time and effort is required to earn someone's trust? How easy is it to betray that trust? Even a small amount of energy in the service of a toxic goal can undo a lifetime of good works. Yoga's eightfold path lists Yamas as the first limb of yoga. Before we do anything else, the yogis have advised us to learn how to restrain our negative behaviors.

Violence, adultery, lying, and stealing are examples of behaviors that can arise from toxic goals. In each case, the individual may think their goal will accrue to their benefit while acknowledging that it will be at the expense of someone else. For a selfish person, this may seem like a win. However, that is only in the short term. The price they pay for their actions is carried forward for the rest of their life: lower self-esteem, damaged reputation, damage to their social network, and, most insidiously, damage to the whole.

From the moon, looking back, it is evident that humans have more in common than separates us. It seems evident that all of humanity shares a small planet. Anything that damages the whole diminishes us all.

The Razor's Edge

In 1946, Somerset Maugham wrote *The Razor's Edge*. The title refers to a phenomenon associated with the spiritual path. The idea is that the spiritual path is broad and easy to start down. But the further you follow this path, the higher you climb, the narrower and more demanding the way becomes. Until, at last, you are walking on the razor's edge.

During a mediocre performance, a mistake is hardly noticeable. At the highest level of competition, the smallest mistake can be catastrophic.

Imagine a world-class climber attempting K2. Small mistakes that might go unnoticed on a climbing wall at the gym are often lethal on this mountain. Those who find themselves ascending the "razor's edge," whatever the context, must be sure to identify and weed out even the smallest toxic goal.

Pruning the Dead Wood

Many people find themselves trapped beneath a web of unexamined goals and expectations. Their situation reminds me of

48

Gulliver, who woke up to find himself snared by the Lilliputians with a thousand tiny ropes. Before you add new goals, see if you can identify and release any toxic goals that immobilize you, dissipate your time, and consume your resources.

The best place to start is with goals you have already identified as toxic. We can divide toxic goals into subjectively toxic (toxic for some people, in certain situations) and objectively toxic (harmful for all people in all circumstances). In either case, one of the surest ways to recognize a toxic goal is by its fruits.

Toxic goals poison consciousness, leaving you feeling bored or scared. Goals that feel like you are pushing them, rather than being pulled by them, are harmful. Healthy goals create a healthy consciousness. Understanding what constitutes a toxic goal will make it easier to recognize, and identification is the first step. Eliminating toxic goals from your mind is more complicated, and we will come back to that later.

Eight Subjectively Toxic Goals

To recognize a subjectively toxic goal, we must understand both the goal and the person holding that goal. The toxicity does not lie in the person or the goal, but the relationship between the two. When the relationship is toxic, we must change one or the other.

If we are looking at our own goals, we do not have the option of switching ourselves out, so the only solution is to change the toxic goal for a positive aspiration. In a team situation, such as a work environment, a manager might very well decide to keep the goal and switch out the employees to find a better fit. Remember, this only works with subjectively toxic goals. If the goal is objectively toxic, you need to replace the goal itself.

The following eight types of goals are examples of subjective toxicity:

1) Unrealistic Goals can be subjective and fluid. For instance, someone paralyzed in an accident might choose the goal of walking again.

Depending upon the damage to the nervous system, their surgeon might think the ambition unrealistic. However, the textbooks are peppered with stories of miraculous recoveries. Who is to say what is possible? At best, we are talking probabilities. Norman Vincent Peale advised us to: "Shoot for the moon. Even if you miss, you'll land among the stars." If we focus more on the quality of the journey and less on the destination, insurmountable ambition need not be toxic.

Whether or not a goal is realistic can change over time, so we must occasionally reconsider them. Sometimes unrealistic dreams become possible as the surrounding reality changes and vice versa. For instance, stem cell research gives new hope to many people with paraplegia. Other times, recovery may seem less probable if new imaging technologies reveal additional damage.

So how do we identify a toxically unrealistic goal? You have to look at how you respond to such a goal. For instance, one person might be so invested in walking again that they resist any rehab that focuses on using a wheelchair or refuse to retrofit their home with ramps. Another person might see the wheelchair as one step on the road to full recovery.

Perhaps the best rule of thumb is that if the person pursuing a goal believes it is possible, and the goal is helping them move forward, the goal may be serving them well, at least for the time being. Later, if they lose hope of walking, they will need to release what has become a toxic goal. Holding onto a goal that you do not believe in is toxic. Often people cling to a goal, not because they still believe in the goal, but out of denial and fear for what the future holds for them. This denial does nothing to help them move forward and postpones the real work of choosing realistic goals and pursuing them vigorously.

2) Outgrown Goals are common, especially with children and young adults. Sometimes there is pressure from others or self-imposed, to stick with a goal. There are times when it is vital to double down,

especially when things get hard. But other times, the goal is toxic and must be abandoned. The only way to know which is to examine the reasons for quitting. If the reason for quitting is boredom or fear, the Flow model can help turn the corner. On the other hand, if the reason is that you have outgrown the goal, then it makes little sense to pursue it.

Imagine a young man who decides that he wants to play for the NFL. Then he finds out that his hero is retiring early due to a concussion. As he finds out more about the post-concussion syndrome, he begins to lose interest in playing professional football and becomes fascinated with the scientists trying to help these athletes.

By now, especially if he has any football talent, there might be considerable pressure from family, team, coaches, community, and not least himself, to hold onto the goal of playing football. After all, only losers quit! If he recognizes his priorities have shifted and dares to correct his course accordingly, he is more likely to succeed in creating the life he wants. Now he can examine his options, including using football to get a scholarship to a school with a good biology program as he pursues a career in neuroscience.

3) Externally Imposed Goals are easy to recognize as toxic. We often spontaneously resist being told our goals, whether by a parent, a teacher, or a supervisor. Just because someone tells you what your goal is, you do not have to accept it. Never let others set your goals for you. A supervisor once told me my job was to recycle the pills returned by nurses to the hospital pharmacy. I soon found that this was tedious work. Without telling anyone, I decided to choose my own goals to put myself in Flow.

My first goal was to break the (imaginary) pharmacy speed record for finishing this job. I timed myself and each day tried to beat my previous record. After a few days of this, boredom and exhaustion caught up with me. So I chose a new goal – to make the job fun! Over time this evolved into a new art form: creating colorful mosaic patterns while sorting pills. Later, I decided to focus on improving the efficiency of my job. After that, I chose to perform my job with good posture, alignment, and fluid movements (as if I was practicing tai chi).

You always have the power to choose what your goals will be, even at work. Never accept a goal from others. Choose your own goals to put yourself in Flow. One of Flow's miracles is that you will perform any task at a higher level of competence.

4) Legacy Goals are inherited. These are goals that are important to your parents, grandparents, or part of a family tradition. Because these goals come from people close to you and perhaps even raised you, they may have been introduced at a very early age and can have a powerful influence on your life. My parents never told me that I had to go to college. They did not have to. It was just assumed! I remember my father telling me that every male MacInerney for the past five generations had graduated from college. Both my parents went to college. My older brother and both sisters went to college. It never occurred to me that I had a choice!

The pressure I felt from my parents was almost insignificant to what I see in some families. The pressure from family can be excessive, sometimes even crushing. It is easy to respond to external pressure with either a modified fight/flight or freeze reaction in such a situation. Some choose to fight, actively rebelling, and often decide to go 180 degrees against their parents' wishes. Some choose flight, taking the path of least resistance, and ending up living the life their parents wanted for them to escape their parents. Some freeze, determining failure is preferable to manifesting someone else's dream. All three strategies are toxic and distract us from the search for personally meaningful goals.

Regarding the pressure I felt to become a physicist, I chose a combination of flight and freeze. I enrolled in university and spent almost four years chasing a degree in physics. I had a natural talent for the subject (as mentioned, my father taught physics) and did not want to hurt my parents' feelings. Despite good grades, I lacked the motivation required to excel, so I changed my major to mathematics. I soon recognized that this was no solution and changed my major to English to become a lawyer. A few months interning with a law firm cured me of that delusion.

I became quite accomplished at identifying what I did not want to do with my life, but I still had no clue what I liked. I felt myself marching toward a degree, a job, and a destiny I no longer desired. So, I froze. With 110 hours of credits and two semesters of Spanish short of a degree, I dropped out of college. I had no idea of who I was or who I wanted to be.

I spent several difficult years working in jobs that did not pay well and that I hated. Eventually, I realized that what I enjoyed most was sharing my love of yoga with friends and family. Pursuing what J. Krishnamurti called "Right Livelihood," I became a yoga teacher. As I developed a clear and compelling vision of how I wanted to live, and aligned my goals and actions around that vision, my relationship with the world began to shift. In the words of Joseph Campbell, "Follow your bliss, and the universe will open doors for you where there were only walls."

Of the three reactions to pressure to take up a legacy goal, be especially careful about the fight reaction. It is easy to delude yourself that you are exerting your own will by defying the expectations of those around you. If your parents tell you to go north, but you teach them a lesson by going south instead, your life is still not your own. You did not even consider going east or north by northwest. You gave up the freedom to choose for yourself in favor of rebelling. The secret is to ignore the pressure and choose from all available options, even if that choice is due north or due south - as long as it is your genuine desire.

Many of us resist advice from others, regardless of whether the advice is good or not. My father was often called a "Master Teacher" by colleagues and administrators. Growing up, adults often asked if

I planned on becoming a teacher like my father. By the time I left home for college, I had no clue what I wanted, but I was pretty sure that I did not want to become a teacher.

Many years later, a retired high school teacher studying with me to become a yoga instructor wrote a testimonial referring to me as a "Master Teacher." I realized that my attempts to evade my father's footsteps had inadvertently led me right into them.

How can you recognize an inherited goal? Ask yourself, if you were to drop this goal or fail to complete it, who would be most disappointed – you or others? If you realize that your real goal is to win someone else's admiration, decide if this is a goal that you want to pursue. If so, check to see if your current course of action is the best plan for winning that approval. Then figure out how to find your Flow in the pursuit of this goal.

On the other hand, if you realize that seeking someone's approval or respect is a toxic goal for you, then drop it and choose a healthier plan to pursue.

5) Cultural Goals are similar to legacy goals in that we inherit them from an outside source. Some cultures have strong expectations that members comply with core values. Examples might be Catholicism's stance against divorce, Jewish dietary restrictions, or Hindu's arranging marriages for their children. Any deviation from these cultural norms can be met with verbal disapproval or, in extreme cases, even physical violence. For those lucky enough to be supported by family and friends, you must still deal with the displeasure of the culture in which you live. If you do not have this support from those you love, it is much worse.

It takes great courage to align with your vision when it does not conform to cultural expectations. As difficult as it might be to escape the tyranny of familial expectations, it is even harder to transcend cultural norms. For some, relocating to a more supportive culture is the only path to freedom.

The most devious cultural goals are those specifically created and planted in your consciousness by experts for their clients' profit. Governments make use of propaganda and corporations of advertising.

The advertising industry spent 223 billion dollars in the U.S. in 2018 to tell us what we want. Often, they create desire out of thin air. If advertising did not work, they would not spend this much money. Most of us are trapped by desires and goals that are the direct result of sophisticated external manipulation. These can blur and overlap with cultural and familial goals.

Before World War II, diamond rings made up only 10% of engagement ring sales. In 1938, the advertising firm of N.W. Ayer convinced Americans that the only way to show your love was to spend two months' salary on a diamond engagement ring. In a few short years, diamond rings accounted for 85-90% of the U.S. engagement ring market.

Some couples start in debt to the jewelers before they have even taken their vows. Although these goals (when ignored) seldom result in violence, they are nevertheless so pervasive that they can be hard to spot, and we dance to their strings without even suspecting that the dance is not our own.

College is another example. For those driven by curiosity or the pursuit of a profession, college may be a necessary and excellent stepping stone on their journey. But many students are just chasing a piece of paper that they believe will improve their earning power as adults. Studies citing the increased earning potential of college graduates over their lifespan can be compelling at first glance. One such study showed that college graduates' annual salary, on average, is three times more than high school dropouts and twice as much as high school graduates. But with a little consideration, you will realize that these studies are fatally flawed because they do not consider other variables like I.Q., E.Q., self-control, lost income, and accumulate debt from delayed entry into the workforce.

On average, college graduates have a higher I.Q. when compared to high school dropouts. College graduates have demonstrated an ability to follow through on projects, compared to high school dropouts. Finally, college graduates probably have better emotional intelligence and mental health, on average, than high school dropouts.

Maybe success has more to do with intelligence, perseverance, emotional and mental health than a college certificate hanging on the wall. What would we find if we compared high school dropouts with good emotional intelligence, who are hardworking and have an I.Q. of 120, with college graduates having the same attributes?

Imagine a kid who loves working outdoors and drops out of high school to work as a landscaper. By their 21st birthday, they could easily have four years of experience and money in the bank. Being debt free, they can afford to wait for the right opportunity to start their own landscaping company. If they land a couple of big contracts and hire more employees, they could be well on their way to being a millionaire by the time they are 30.

Compare them to the student who goes to college to make a higher salary upon graduating. After four years, they graduate. Even if they have a marketable degree like engineering, they are still faced with debt and cannot afford to wait for the right job to come along, nor can they afford to gamble on starting their own business. Instead, they will most likely take the first job that helps them start paying off school debt. This type of job may not pay as well, and even with good performance, there will probably be a ceiling on earning potential.

Meanwhile, they have taken on more debt with a new car, wardrobe, and a few years later, maybe even marriage, kids, and a house. They are still trying to pay off college debt. They have few options and cannot afford to walk away. Employers know that they can pay such an employee less, work them harder, and treat them worse than other employees who can afford to quit.

One of the benefits of traveling to foreign countries is that you realize that there is more than one way to live a happy and meaningful life. For those unable or unwilling to travel, literature can have a similar effect, especially when set in unfamiliar cultures or historical periods.

To filter for cultural goals, ask yourself the following. If you lived in a foreign country, would that change your dream? If so, you might want to take a closer look at the cultural pressures that might be negatively influencing your choices.

"He who joyfully marches in rank and file has already earned my contempt. He has been given a large brain by mistake, since for him the spinal cord would suffice." - Albert Einstein.

6) Flow Preventing Goals are always toxic. When the balance between goals and skills is lost, resulting in boredom or anxiety, we must notice, erase attachment to the old goal, and replace it with something better.

Discard boring goals to make room for more challenging goals. As your skill level increases in the pursuit of a goal, scary goals become less threatening, while boring goals become only more boring. Raise the bar enough to make it enjoyable, or consider replacing the goal altogether.

Scary goals are okay in some circumstances. If the goal meets all of the other qualifications of a good plan but causes you anxiety, do not jettison it immediately. Instead, break the goal down into smaller and more manageable steps, and then choose an intermediary step that is not scary. Find Flow, and practice until you are ready to take the next step. Keep your focus on what you are doing and the immediate next step. Looking too far ahead often results in anxiety.

Boredom and fear relate to the speed at which you are implementing strategy. When bored, speed up your progress taking larger steps more frequently. When anxious, slow down or even back up temporarily, and then move forward with smaller, less frequent steps.

7) Dissipating Goals pull in a similar direction but distract your focus from the one true goal. Often dissipating goals are not chosen consciously. They creep in unbidden and steal energy from the purpose that is most important to you. Choose one goal. Then erase any attachment to the other distracting goals, and redirect that energy into the most crucial

goal, as you pursue that goal with focused determination! Beware, dissipative goals can creep back in unnoticed. If they return, root them out repeatedly until you are free to focus with full attention on what is important to you.

8) Tangential Goals may pass all of the previous tests and still be toxic. They may be of your choosing, positive, creative, put you in Flow, and still be harmful. Any goal that pulls you away from your highest vision, sabotaging your aspirations, is toxic. You have limited time, energy, and money. Learn to recognize tangents that may be fun, pleasant or exciting, but ultimately distract you from more important and pressing goals.

Imagine you are in a relationship with someone whose goals pull you away from your aspirations. You need to take a close look at your priorities. If the desire for a healthy connection with this person is more important than your personal goals, then make the relationship your focus, and recognize that some of your old goals may be toxic. On the other hand, if your life goals are more important to you than the relationship, then the relationship must evolve to accommodate your highest aspirations or consider ending the relationship.

Eight Objectively Toxic Goals

Some goals are toxic in and of themselves, regardless of the individual or their circumstance. We will examine each of these in more detail.

1) External Locus of Control Goals refers to goals that you do not have the power to manifest. For example, getting a promotion at work may not be within your locus of control if the decision resides with a boss who may or may not be fair-minded. When your success or failure is dependent upon the actions of others, so is your self-esteem. When you realize that you have a goal with an external locus of control, see if you can convert it into an internal locus of control. Rather than trying to win a promotion at work (where success and failure depend upon others' decisions), instead set out to demonstrate to your boss that you are worthy of that promotion. Measure success or failure by the quality of your performance (which you have control over) rather than your boss's decision (which you do not control).

If you have done your best but fail to get the promotion, you can still take pride in having met your goal. Perhaps your boss, seeing how hard you worked to get the job she gave to someone else and how gracefully you adapted to her decision, will put you at the top of her list for a future position. Especially when compared to the person who fixated on getting the job and, when denied, throws a temper tantrum, sulks, or otherwise displays infantile behavior.

If you cannot convert a goal into an internal locus of control, consider discarding the goal altogether. If you are unwilling to discard such a goal, be sure to watch that it does not become the source of pain and suffering in your life or for those around you.

I recommend keeping goals with an external locus of control to a minimum. They can easily tie you down, leave you vulnerable and disempowered.

When evaluating whether the locus of control is external or internal, keep in mind that this depends not only on the goal but also on whose goal it is. For instance, when setting a company goal, like decreasing on-the-job injuries, the question is not whether it is in your ability to do so, but whether it is within the company's ability to do so.

2) Self-destructive Goals can arise from various sources, including guilt, self-loathing, fear, or boredom. By definition, these goals do not serve you well and can be considered toxic. They are easy to see in others but can be harder to see in yourself. The mindset that generates this kind of goal is not conducive to self-inquiry, awareness, compassion, or self-love. Even when you intellectually identify such goals, they can still be challenging to escape.

Often a self-destructive goal is a means to an end. It might be a cry for help or an attempt to distract from, avoid or escape something worse. Some people use diets or exercise to punish themselves. Others work late to avoid facing problems at home. Some people take on the role of victim to gain attention.

Self-destructive goals might feel like they serve a purpose, but this behavior is a dead-end in the long run. It takes courageous self-inquiry to identify issues or ideas you have been avoiding. If you can see through to the root of the real problem, self-destructive goals often fall away of their own accord and can be replaced with higher aspirations that promote self-healing.

3) Selfish Goals may seem to benefit you in the short term, but it is at the expense of your relationships over the long term. When you pursue such goals, lovers, family, friends, pets, colleagues, society, or the environment pay the price. Over time, you, too, are harmed. In damaging your relationships, you damage your larger self. Living as a parasite, deriving benefit at the expense of the whole leads to a loss of self-esteem and, carried to its logical extension, results in self-loathing. Replace such goals with symbiotic objectives, where all parties derive benefit. For instance, moving your family so that you can pursue a new job might or might not be ideal for your spouse and children. It can be helpful to discuss such decisions with those most affected. Suppose each family member identifies the pros and cons of the move from a personal perspective and puts forward options for the group to consider. It may take a little longer, but you are more likely to find a solution that everyone can support in the end.

4) Negative Goals define failure and then seek to avoid it. These goals are objectively toxic. They generate boredom when there is no threat of failure and fear when there is. Even worse, they have a propensity for manifesting the very failure they seek to avert. Imagine climbing a tall tree, focused on reaching the top branch to recover your brand-new camera drone. Then you look down, and suddenly you have a new goal… "Don't fall and break your neck!" This goal is instantly and objectively toxic and creates anxiety. Fear destroys balance, drains strength from muscles, and clouds judgment. The goal of not falling makes falling more likely! This is a textbook example of a toxic goal. What advice do experienced climbers give the newbies? "Don't look down!" This advice is not only appropriate when clinging to the side of a mountain, but it applies equally well to life.

5) Status Quo Goals are common, taken for granted, and seldom questioned. And yet, they are objectively toxic, replacing Flow with boredom and fear. For instance, the goal of keeping the money you already have is a status quo goal. If nothing threatens your money, you are bored. If something is threatening to take your money, you are anxious. When you identify a status quo goal, erase it, and redirect that energy toward creating a future that inspires Flow. We will take a closer look at status quo goals in the next chapter.

6) Nostalgic Goals result from dissatisfaction with the status quo and seeks a return to "better" times. Older populations have a natural predisposition to sentimentality. However, it is impossible to turn back time. The best you can hope for is to create an isolated bubble where the past lives on as a museum. Such fantasies can be comforting to indulge, but they dissipate time and energy that you could be using to build a better future.

7) Shadow Goals are similar to negative goals, except you do not consciously choose them. A strong desire often casts a shadow, generating a strong aversion to its opposite. For instance, you may start with the positive goal of wanting to win a tennis game. Without realizing it, this desire to win can develop a shadow goal - an aversion

to losing. If you are trying not to fail, you are thinking about failure rather than success. You measure yourself against this standard of failure. The original goal may have been healthy, but its shadow goal is not! If you are not careful, the shadow goal will replace the initial intent with all of the consequences that negative goals bring. If you notice a shadow goal has surfaced, erase it immediately. Then redirect your attention and energy to the pursuit of the original, positive goal.

8) Subversive Goals are perhaps the most important and overlooked toxic goals. They are often buried deep in the psyche and can cause great harm. These goals work to sabotage and undermine your conscious aspirations. Imagine you are com-

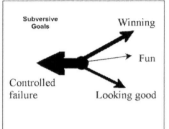

peting in a tennis match. In the diagram at right, notice that winning, having fun, and looking good all pull in slightly different directions, weakening your performance. By having multiple goals, you are not able to fully commit to any single objective. Thus, performance suffers. However, because these goals all pull in a similar direction, their negative effect is diminished. Now, look at the arrow pointing to the left! Even the slightest bit of energy devoted to sabotaging performance can be catastrophic. When swinging at a 98 mph fastball, how much negative energy does it take to convert a home run into an easy popup?

Why would anyone ever sabotage their dreams? The most common answer is that they suffer from an unconscious fear of success.

Marianne Williamson expressed this idea most eloquently when she wrote, "Our deepest fear is not that we are inadequate. Our deepest fear is that we are powerful beyond measure. It is our light, not our darkness that most frightens us. We ask ourselves, 'Who am I to be brilliant, gorgeous, talented, fabulous?' Actually, who are you not to be? You are a child of God."

What is it about success that scares us? There are several possible answers to this question, one or all of which might apply to you. Success is unpredictable. Even if I could guarantee my performance, I cannot ensure success. There are too many moving parts, including the conduct of colleagues, competitors, an inopportune sneeze, and other acts of God! Striving for perfect results makes you more vulnerable. It confronts you with the reality that you are never entirely in control of your success.

Mediocrity, on the other hand, is predictable. I can deliver mediocrity at will. The desire to always be in control of outcomes (a claustrophobic delusion) will inevitably steer you away from manifesting your full potential. You will find yourself holding back something for a rainy day. But power is grown by exercising it, not hoarding it.

Perhaps your fear of success stems from a fear of making mistakes? Everyone makes mistakes! A small life risks small mistakes, whereas a larger life plays with higher stakes. During the last part of World War II, General Eisenhower had to decide whether to launch D-Day, the allied invasion of Normandy, France. The lives of millions of people and the outcome of the war were on his shoulders. It turned out well for the Allies, but while wrestling with this decision, Eisenhower knew that catastrophic failure was a real possibility. If you want to minimize the consequences of a mistake, you will tend to lean into the predictability of mediocrity, often without realizing it.

If you suffer from excessive imagination, you may find that you fear the consequences of an error more than the actual error. It is easy to become immobilized by the weight of these unseen, unknowable ramifications.

Imagine you own a business. Faced with going out of business, you decide to modernize your equipment. One of your employees loses their position in the process. Because this employee was already stretched thin on a mortgage, they lose their home. Moving to a cheaper but crime-ridden area of town, they watch as their teenage son falls in with a violent peer group. It is easy to carry guilt into the distant future. At what point are the consequences of your original action no longer your responsibility? How much blame do you share for the future actions of your employee's son?

Now imagine that you purchase health insurance for your remaining employees with the money you save from modernizing your plant. How much credit do you deserve for unforeseen positive consequences? One employee becomes sick, but because she is insured, she gets treatment and recovers. The next year she gives birth to a healthy daughter, who grows up to become a biochemist, and finds a cure for breast cancer. As you spin out the potentials for positive and negative outcomes, you can become lost in a hall of mirrors.

As you explore more profound states of Flow, your performance will naturally improve, sometimes miraculously. Those around you may sing your praises. You may even start to listen and believe what they say about you. The sleeping ego awakens and proclaims, "Look what I did!" But it was in the absence of "self" that the miraculous occurred. You are, at best, a witness to your experience of Flow, never its source. Taking credit for successful outcomes leads to pride, and similar destructive emotions, when things are going well. Taking responsibility for negative results leads to humiliation, embarrassment, regret, and other negative emotions. If you feel yourself shrinking from the dream of living a larger life, recognize that it may be fear talking to you rather than common sense. Listen to the message fear brings to your attention, but do not make decisions or act out of fear.

Several millennia ago, yogis recognized that Deep Flow often aroused ego with predictable results. Their solution can be found in the second limb of yoga (Niyamas or observances) and is called Ishvara Pranidhana. In the Upanishads, Ishvara translates as "a state of collective consciousness," but often, you will see the word "God" or "Lord" substituted. Pranidhana means surrender or support. Ishvara Pranidhana translates as surrendering your life to God (Universe, collective consciousness, most authentic self, etc.). Some prefer to think of this as supporting and being supported by the collective consciousness. Another standard translation is "dedication of the fruits of your actions to the Lord."

In the Christian Bible, we can find a similar idea: "Thy will be done." The basic idea is that we do our best but leave the outcome in God's hands. There are three levels to this insight. First, performance comes from a deeper source than the ego, which rises to accept credit. Second, your actions exist in a complex web of interactions with the universe, which gives rise to results. These results are not yours to claim. Third, there is no way for us to judge whether the results are good or bad.

Take the illustration of the farmer and his mare. A farmer has a beautiful mare that comes when he whistles! Is this a good thing or bad? His wonderful mare runs off into the mountains. Is this a good thing or bad? He later finds his mare running with a stallion. When he whistles, she comes, and the stallion follows them back to the farm. Is this a good thing or bad? His son tries to break-in the stallion and is thrown and breaks his leg. Is this a good thing or bad? War breaks out, and all the young men in the valley are drafted, except the farmer's son. Is this a good thing or bad?

I am sure you have long since gotten the point of this story, but that does not diminish its importance. We cannot possibly tell fortune from misfortune. Why do we spend so much time and energy judging every event or possible action? Imagine how much more we could accomplish if we took that time and energy and redirected it toward a positive goal.

Focus on the present moment and let the future take care of itself. Do not take pride in an apparent success or feel ashamed of so-called failure. To the degree that you can live by these precepts, you will enjoy serenity of spirit. You will not be immobilized by indecision, trying to foresee the unforeseeable.

The greatest gift of Ishvara Pranidhana is that it helps us to stay in Deep Flow. When the miraculous abounds and ego stirs, rededicate the fruits of your labor to your concept of God, the infinite or collective consciousness.

"If you can meet with triumph and disaster and treat those two impostors just the same…" - from Rudyard Kipling's poem, "If"

There is one more reason we might succumb to subversive goals. You might fear the spotlight. Being known or famous is like pouring gasoline on a lit match. Any slight pain, embarrassment, or humiliation is instantly amplified and bounced around the echo chamber of public opinion. Much safer to stay well hidden under a rock.

Decide how much success you want or can stand, but do not choose out of fear. Be clear on your answer, then live accordingly. It is when people think they want one thing but actually want the opposite that tragedy ensues. One person thinks she wants fame until she gets it. Another person thinks he wants obscurity, but in time comes to regret the decisions that led him there.

The Art of Voluntary Simplicity

"Besides the noble art of getting things done, there is the noble art of leaving things undone. The wisdom of life consists in the elimination of non-essentials." ~ Lin Yutang

Sometimes "successful" people wake up to discover they are slaves to their success. They spend an increasing portion of their time protecting and maintaining their investments, home, and possessions. Success tends toward complexity, and complexity adds to stress. Soon they are too busy chasing their tails in circles to ask fundamental questions like, "What do I want in life?" and "What is most important to me?" Then they fall ill from stress and are too tired to ask such critical questions. At the very end, when most of us do ask these questions, there is seldom enough time to answer or act on those answers.

There is a small but growing trend of people who turn their backs on lifestyles centered on consumption and complexity, preferring to embrace a new paradigm of voluntary simplicity. Even as India and third-world cultures stampede toward the Western materialistic life-style, people are beginning to look for simpler, more spiritual ways of living here in the West.

This quest for simplicity applies not just to our lifestyle but equally to internal states of mind. Even a billionaire can lay awake in bed at 3 a.m., drowning in the complexity of his thoughts. We think we want greater freedom and more options, not fewer. In truth, you, like most modern humans, probably suffer from too many choices, rather than too few.

No one asked the blacksmith's son what he wanted to do in the Middle Ages when he grew up. Life used to be simpler. Now we are exhausted from too much choice. Even a visit to an ice cream shop has become an exercise in complexity.

"There is no mystery attached to the fact that, in this new era in human history, when for the first time, large numbers of people can live unconstrained lives involving high levels of choice, there is a concurrent explosion in depression rates. The burden of responsibility for making innumerable choices can result in a person's becoming psychologically tyrannized by them." ~ Gregg D. Jacobs

The desire for simplicity is at the heart of the growing popularity of meditation. I invite you to consider practicing voluntary simplicity regarding your mind, and specifically, concerning your goals. This may not be easy to do, but the rewards are substantial.

When you hold onto all possibilities, you end up manifesting none of them. You find yourself immobilized by a thousand invisible goals, pulling you in a thousand different directions, stuck like a fly in a web of your own making. Eliminate toxic goals, commit to healthier aspirations, and perform with Flow.

The Fifth Column

Of all the toxic goals, subversive goals are often the most challenging to expunge. Self-destructive goals have the potential to do great harm, but this also makes them easier to spot. On the other hand, subversive goals work quietly, beneath the surface like termites, eating away just enough to undermine but not cripple your dreams.

To help you get a better feel for subversive goals, I include two examples from my own experience that illustrate how and why such goals originate. In my junior year of college, I was warming up in the racquetball courts the night before a big tournament. Two competitors from out of town were already on the court and offered to let me warm up with them in a cutthroat match.

Twenty minutes into the game, I slipped into a Deep Flow experience. All effort fell away. The less I tried, the harder I hit the ball. I was splitting balls in two, almost at will. After going through three balls, I eased up on power and focused on control. Every time I swung; I rolled the ball off the front wall along the floor. Then I started using pinch shots, ceiling shots, and triple wall shots off the back wall that rolled off the front wall. Each stroke was perfect. I moved the other two players around the court like chess pieces. I was not thinking, just witnessing, and caught up in the Flow. It felt more like a fluid underwater dance. Time slowed down. After 30 minutes of this, the other two players quit the court in disgust. On the drive home, every traffic light turned green as I approached.

The next morning, I woke up and realized that I was still in Flow! I arrived at the hosting racquetball club for the first day of the tournament. I had never been in Flow during competition and knew that I was playing well enough to easily win the tournament or any tournament, for that matter.

As I approached the court for my first match, I saw a small crowd of players gathered. One of the players from the previous night pointed at me and said, "There he is. That's the one we were telling you about." A crowd gathered in the balcony to watch my match. I felt my stomach tighten with anxiety as I realized that they were here to see magic. I knew that I did not know how to repeat what had happened the previous night. It was the absence of "I" that allowed the Deep Flow. But now, "I" was entirely in charge. Before this expectant audience, I delivered a master class in mediocrity. Gradually (and thankfully), the gallery cleared, many shaking their heads, embarrassed for me. I won the match through attrition and crashed out of the tournament in the second round.

Deep Flow is impressive to watch and incredible to experience. We hold onto the memory of such moments throughout our lives. But falling from Deep Flow to mediocrity is painful, especially for the ego. If you do not want to experience such pain, which is understandable, you need to be consistent. It is impossible to be consistently brilliant but relatively easy to be consistently mediocre.

Subversive goals keep us safe by tamping down the highs. Just a little nudge is all that it takes to turn miraculous into predictable. It is the fear of success that gives rise to the subversive goal of mediocrity. The secret to escaping this trap is first to see it. If your goal is emotional security, mediocrity may be the solution in the short run, but it leads to a life of regret in the long run. If you want to touch Deep Flow now and then, you have to keep that front and center and be willing occasionally to experience catastrophic failure in your pursuit of the miraculous.

Several years after that racquetball tournament, I dropped out of college and found a job as a hospital pharmacy technician. It was hard work, repetitive, boring, and essential! Mistakes were not permitted. A dozen of us rotated through the same job, and management timed us to measure our performance against each other and our past performance.

One day I was in a great mood, full of energy, and everything was clicking. I realized that I was on track to finish my assigned morning tasks almost an hour ahead of schedule. A little voice woke up inside of me. It cautioned that if I continued to perform at this level today, my co-workers and management would expect me to work this hard every day and increase my workload. Listening to this voice, I deliberately slowed down. Where I had been enjoying my work that morning, I was now bored, and time dragged. The last hour felt longer than the previous three hours.

One of my fellow technicians, Walter, always seemed to give his all at work. When he finished early, he would offer to help slower workers or ask management for an extra assignment. He always seemed to enjoy his work. He gave every appearance of being in Flow. One day he came into work hungover from a night of partying. One look was enough for the rest of us to feel his pain. My impulse was strong and immediate, as was that of the other technicians and pharmacists. How can we help? We all worked harder to finish our assignments in time to help Walter get through the morning.

As I worked alongside Walter, I saw how others responded to his suffering and my impulse to help. I realized that the voice that cautioned me to pursue mediocrity had lied to me.

Soon after this epiphany, I started a new job. I saw this as an opportunity to turn over a new leaf. I vowed to find my own "inner Walter," and seek my highest performance every time, in the knowledge that sometimes I would soar and other times I might crash. But in each case, I would be shooting for gold.

In his famous essay, "Self-Reliance," Ralph Waldo Emerson wrote, "A foolish consistency is the hobgoblin of little minds, adored by little statesmen and philosophers and divines. With consistency, a great soul has simply nothing to do. He may as well concern himself with his shadow on the wall."

Letting Go of Toxic Goals

"Habits are first cobwebs, then cables." - Spanish proverb.

My uncle once told me how they used to catch raccoons when he was a boy growing up poor on a small farm in the Appalachians. "We would drill a hole into a log, wider at the bottom, narrower at the top. Then we would drop a shiny marble into the hole. Raccoons can't pass up a shiny marble. They would reach into the hole and grab the marble but couldn't pull their hand out of the log without first letting go of the marble. The next day we would go back, and there was a raccoon waiting for us."

"But why don't they just let go of the marble?" I asked. It seemed so simple to me as a child, let go of the marble and be free! As an adult, I realize that it is not always a simple thing to let go of a desire, even when it causes suffering.

For many, their desires are not even their own. Many of our desires come from others – not just parents and peers. Not only do we accumulate desires and goals mindlessly, but worse, we become attached to these goals and follow them, oblivious to where they might lead. Goals can be fickle. They can turn on us in a variety of ways. I continued to play racquetball long after the doctors and my knees told me to quit. For every athlete who wins an Olympic gold medal, thousands fail along the way. Those who cannot release the objective of winning gold will suffer at the hands of the goal that initially inspired them.

Goals can be powerful tools when used correctly. But a person who does not understand at a deep level what his dreams and desires are and cannot regularly examine, weigh, judge, evaluate, and, if necessary, discard goals that no longer serve is just a marionette dancing on strings.

We are so busy chasing our desires or grieving over unfulfilled expectations that we do not stop to ask

71

some critical questions. Are these goals aligned with our highest values? Do they distract us from more important goals? Are they our own goals, or did we pick them up from someone else along the way? Is there a more direct path to where we want to go?

In our culture, we worship success while denouncing quitters. But even the most casual examination reveals cases in which changing course is infinitely preferable to staying the course. Just ask the raccoon who gave up a marble and lived to tell the tale.

Attachment and aversion are flip sides of the same coin. Both actions strengthen our association with the object in question. Hatred can bind two people together as effectively as love. One of my favorite Buddhist parables deals with this theme. Two monks set out upon a pilgrimage. One day, they came to a riverbank and saw a beautiful girl who could not cross the river. Feeling compassion for her, the elder monk carried her across the river on his back. Meanwhile, the younger one looked on in consternation, remembering the rules of their order to avoid women.

That night, the elder monk quickly fell asleep while the younger one twisted around, unable to calm his mind. Finally, he woke up the older monk and reprimanded him, "As monks, we are supposed to avoid women. I am troubled and ashamed by what you did today." The elder monk looked at his friend and smiled patiently. "Brother, I left the girl behind by the river bank. Why are you still carrying her around?"

Consider a pair of electromagnets. When current pushes through the coils surrounding the magnets, they are attracted to each other. If you reverse the current in one magnet, they repel each other. In either case, whether attracting or repelling, the magnets are affecting each other's behavior. But if you cut the electric current flowing through the magnets' wires, they no longer interact. This is what we must do with our toxic goals. Rather than replace the attachment to a toxic goal with an aversion to that same goal, we must figure out how to "cut the current."

After you have identified a goal that you need to relinquish, first take a close look at it. See it clearly in your head and feel it in your heart. Examine the roots of the goal. Be sure you know what it is you are going to release. Then, on an exhale, let it go. Notice if you feel any differently. With practice, most people will feel a lighter sensation in their body as muscles relax. Then take another breath, and on your exhale, let go of all goals, including your vision. Soften your face, release your shoulders, surrender control of the present moment, and breathe out with a sigh. Think of this step as erasing the blackboard (or reformatting your hard drive). When successful, many students report feeling lighter and more centered.

If you cannot release your attachment to the goal with an exhalation, try one of the following tricks. Draw a symbol, collage, or picture representing your goal or your attachment to that goal. Then set the drawing on fire. As the paper burns, use a long exhalation and release all attachment to the plan. Alternatively, visualize putting the goal in a wicker basket hanging beneath a hot air balloon, which carries the goal away when released. The fact is that you already know how to release a goal. You do it every night as you fall asleep.

A Texas-Sized Ring Cycle

In 1996 Aquarena Springs, a legendary family-owned theme park in San Marcos, Texas, closed down. They were famous for their glass-bottom boats and underwater theatre (complete with mermaids). But the star attraction was Ralph the Diving Pig. Each performance would start with Ralph running down the "volcano ramp" and executing his famous "swine dive" into the spring-fed pool. Its closing marked the passing of an era.

In tribute, Austin's Zachary Scott Theatre performed a parody of Richard Wagner's epic opera 'Der Ring des Nibelungen', otherwise known as The Ring Cycle. They compressed the four individual operas lasting 15 hours into a single 90-minute musical and set it in San Marcos.

They replaced the Rhine Maidens with the Aquarena Mermaids and the swords with Texas six-shooters. The production was full of inside jokes and Texas-sized puns.

I attended a matinee performance with friends. Although most of the audience were adults, in the front row was a group of children with varying disabilities and their chaperones. Some had Down syndrome, others had leg braces, and one was in a wheelchair.

As the performance progressed, it became clear that these kids identified more closely with the misshapen dwarf than with the tall and handsome hero, Siegfried!

As Siegfried prepared to shoot the dwarf at the play's climax, the children were beside themselves. They shouted out warnings to the dwarf. Several even attempted to climb up on stage to intervene.

Everyone in the audience held their breath. The actors exchanged worried glances. Then one of them shrugged. The play resumed with the actors ad-libbing a new ending to the play, recasting the dwarf as the hero. These creative entertainers received a standing ovation from the audience, the children, the chaperones, and even the stage crew.

This performance is a small but perfect example of how a goal (performing the play the way it was written and rehearsed) can unexpectedly become toxic and how fluid goal setting can restore flow. The actors saw what was happening and responded in real-time by embracing a new goal that did not involve traumatizing a group of young and enthusiastic theatergoers.

The trouble with toxic goals is not just letting them go. It is that they return when you are not looking and take up residence again, bringing boredom and fear with them. You cannot defeat a negative goal with another negative goal. In the next chapter, we will see why the attempt to avoid a toxic goal is itself a toxic goal and learn how to employ an alternative approach to dealing with toxic goals that will work.

Chapter Three

THE CIRCLE OF FAILURE

Balance

In 1994, I taught my first workshop on improving balance. I asked the students to stand on one leg. Looking around the room, I saw that most of the students were wobbling back and forth. Those with less balance had larger gyrations. Those with better balance compressed these oscillations into a rigid vibration of tension. Two students looked bored; the rest looked anxious. I enjoy balancing poses, but it was evident that my students did not share the sentiment. Having read about Mihaly Csikszentmihalyi's concepts on Flow, I realized that my students were not in Flow.

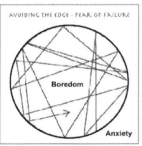

To help these students find their Flow state, I first had to understand their goals and how much skill they brought to the workshop. Skill level was easy to assess; a casual glance around the room sufficed. Understanding someone else's goals is trickier. I started asking my students, as they wobbled back and forth balanced on one foot, "What is your goal?" Most were vague or seemed confused by the question. One replied, "to not fall over." Another student talked about improving alignment. Over the next few months, I asked dozens and then hundreds of students the same question. I was puzzled by their responses or lack of a response. Not a single person gave me the correct answer!

You may be curious how I could have known what a student's goal was even when they didn't. The insight came through careful observation. When they started to fall, most of them kept fighting to keep their balance. They swung their arms and hopped around, fighting to recover, right up to the moment that their raised foot touched the floor. In that instant, I saw their failure in their face and the slump of their shoulders. I heard their disappointment in the sound of their exhalation. The moment they perceived as failure showed me that their real goal was to avoid putting their foot down!

Yet, when I asked these students, "What is your goal?" not a single student mentioned their foot. To make sure I was correct, I followed up by sharing what I thought their goal was. Every student I talked with agreed that not putting their foot down was indeed their true goal, once they thought about it for a moment. However, they had not realized it until I pointed it out to them.

Sometimes, one student would lose their balance, and I would see half the class visibly relax. I was surprised at how many people had the goal of not being the first person to put their foot down.

Sometimes I would ask them, "When you entered the yoga studio, did you say to yourself, 'My goal is not to be the first person to put their foot down'?" They admitted that they did not consciously choose that goal. I came to realize that most of our goals run beneath the surface yet wield great power over our state of mind. This inquiry into the unconscious aspirations that my students brought to class marked the beginning of my fascination with goals and Flow and improving concentration.

Why is the goal of not putting your foot down a toxic goal? Because it is negative! The student has identified what failure looks like and then goes about trying not to fail. I am not implying that yoga students with a negative goal will not improve. Over time, they may get better at not putting their foot down. Instead of a big wobble, they have a small wobble, which becomes a vibration, which gives way to rigidity. But in the set of their face, you still see anxiety or occasionally boredom, never Flow.

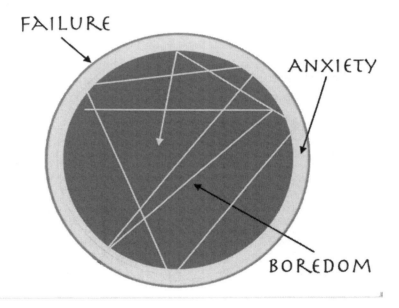

CIRCLE OF FAILURE

FAILURE

ANXIETY

BOREDOM

To help explain what I saw in these balance workshops, I created the model above, which I call the "Circle of Failure" or sometimes the "Circle of Avoidance." In this model, failure is clearly defined (the outer circle), but success is vague (the innermost area). Anywhere inside the perimeter of the circle is equally successful.

Imagine yourself inside the circle. Your goal is not to fail, and you are not failing. Left without a clear objective, you drift. Eventually, you float too close to the edge and see failure looming large. Anxiety replaces boredom. You make an abrupt change of direction to avoid failure. Now you are moving away from the edge. The crisis is averted; you are no longer in danger of failing. So, you go back to sleep, drifting until the next emergency. This kind of goal creates a life of boredom with moments of panic.

Imagine a high school student whose only goal is not to get an F on their report card. Their expectations are set very low. If they have a C average, they are succeeding. There is no motivation to study or work. They ditch school to hang out with the other cool students behind the shop building. They are bored until their C has become a D. Then they get scared and make a radical adjustment to avoid failing. Perhaps they go to the library to study for the next test and do some homework. As they pull away from failure, the crisis passes, and they go back to drifting. They live a life of boredom with moments of panic.

Now, look at the circle on the right side of the diagram. Here, expectations are set higher. The margin of error is smaller, and thus they are never more than a hair's breadth away from failing. They live with the possibility of failure, continually making course corrections to avert disaster. They live a life of anxiety with rare moments of boredom.

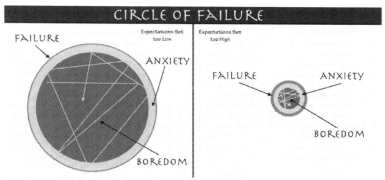

Imagine a high school student whose goal is to get straight A's on their report card. If you ask them, "Is this a positive goal?" they

probably will say yes. But for most of them, it is a negative goal. They mean that they do not want anything less than straight A's, and a B is considered a failure. Their real motivation is not to fail. By setting their standards so high, they contract their circle of failure. It is harder to avoid a B than to avoid an F. This student is continuously worried about failing, and for a good reason! One mistake is all it takes to ruin a straight-A report card. They suffer from stress most of the time, but on the rare occasion that their grades are secure, they lack any further motivation to continue studying. They live a life of anxiety interspersed with rare periods of boredom.

Negative goals define failure and then seek to avoid it. In so doing, they destroy Flow and replace it with varying degrees of boredom and fear, depending upon how high or low expectations are set. In this model, success is vague, and failure is clearly defined, which, more often than not, results in manifesting the very failure that they seek to avoid. It is easier to appreciate this if you look at a few examples.

Steve defines a successful marriage as one in which his wife Suzie does not leave him (a negative goal). To start with, Suzie has no plans to leave him, so he has no motivation. Steve spends the evenings drinking beer, watching football, and playing poker with the guys. If he behaves this way long enough, he comes home to find Suzie packing her bags. Losing his wife was the very thing he did not want to happen. Steve makes an abrupt course correction to avoid failure. He buys her roses and chocolates, maybe even takes her out to dinner. She decides to give him a second chance and unpacks. Now that the crisis is averted, he has no direction, so he goes back to his old patterns. A marriage of boredom with moments of panic, until the unthinkable happens, and Suzie does not come back. Steve's attempt to avoid failure is, in large part, responsible for manifesting that failure!

Monica is training as a gymnast. Last year, Monica was fearless on the equipment and loved the competition. Her coach held out the hope that she might make the national team in a few years if she kept improving. Then Monica saw her friend Rachel take a nasty fall on the balance beam, suffering a concussion and breaking her collar bone. The next time Suzie mounts the balance beam, she has a new goal: not breaking her neck. This goal is negative. It replaces the Flow with fear. Fear causes her muscles to tense, destroys her balance, and increases the chance of injury. If she cannot control her goals and regain Flow, any future as a gymnast is lost, and the smartest thing she can do is quit the sport before she is seriously injured.

Think back to our earlier discussion on how to open your Flow window. Remember how some people hate boredom so much that they go out of their way to avoid it. They consistently choose challenging situations over boring ones. As they become more adept at handling fear, they do not open their Flow window. They just shift it upward. The person who hates feeling scared so much that they always choose boredom over fear ends up moving their Flow window down. One attempts to avoid fear and ends up living a life dominated by fear. One attempts to avoid boredom and ends up living a life dominated by boredom. Either case amounts to a tragic waste of life.

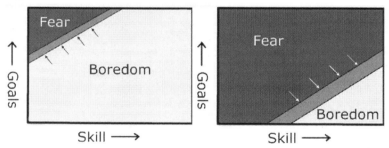

There are at least three reasons why negative goals and the Circle of Failure manifest failure. If your goal is not to fail, you will do just enough to avoid failure, then lose interest until the next crisis. You are always just one step away from failure. It is only a matter of time before chocolate and Flowers are not enough to avert disaster.

The second problem with negative goals is that they replace Flow with boredom or fear. When you're bored or scared, you are more likely to make mistakes. And seeing as you are only a few steps away from failing, any error can push you over the edge.

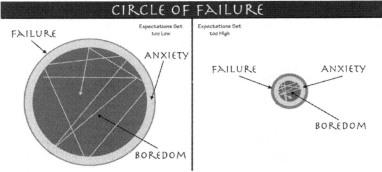

The third reason is that your subconscious mind does not process negative words like "don't." When Monica tells herself, "don't fall and break your neck," she is filling her mind with images of failure, drawing her attention away from success.

This pattern of negative goals manifesting failure is so common that once you learn to identify it, you will find examples of it in your friends, colleagues, and family. The real trick is to see it in yourself. Learn to replace any negative goals with positive alternatives. In the next chapter, we will discuss how to go about doing this.

Chapter Four

THE BLUE DOT OF SUCCESS

"Obstacles are those frightful things you see when you take your eyes off your goal." ~ Henry Ford

What Makes a Goal Positive?

We have talked at length about what constitutes a negative goal. Now, let us consider what makes a goal positive. I was talking to a group of University of Texas students about the Circle of Failure. Pointing to the red circle, I asked, "If this is a circle of failure, what does this represent?" Then I drew a blue dot on the opposite side of the whiteboard.

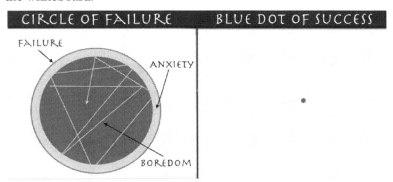

A student from the back of the room called out, "The Blue Dot of Success!" and I have been using that name ever since. The Blue Dot represents a clear and inspiring goal. With a positive goal, you have nothing to lose and everything to gain. Having nothing to lose, you are fearless. Having everything to gain, you are never bored. Negative goals destroy Flow, and positive goals create Flow. It is that simple.

I pointed to the red circle and said, "If this circle represents failure, where is failure represented in this model?" as I gestured to the opposite side of the whiteboard. I was waiting for someone to shout out, "Failure does not exist!" Instead, a young woman gestured to the Blue Dot and pronounced that everything outside the Blue Dot represented failure. I knew she was wrong but struggled to explain why.

Eventually, I hit upon the following example. Imagine a seven-year-old girl whose "Blue Dot of Success" is to grow up to become an astronaut. If you ask her if she is already an astronaut, she might reply, "Not yet, I am only seven" and probably roll her eyes at your stupid question. The idea that because she is not already an astronaut, she is failing in her goal to become one makes no sense. Even a seven-year-old child knows that. Positive goals are never about what you already have but rather what you hope to gain in the future.

In the Blue Dot of Success model, failure does not exist. You must grasp this principle. Thoughts about failure and success compete for oxygen. The more you focus on success, the less energy is available to dwell on defeat. Likewise, the more you focus on the negative, the less energy is available for success.

Think back to any outstanding athletic performance. Do you think the gymnast was giving any thought to trying not to fail as she lined up for her dismount? Or the batter was praying, "Please don't let me strikeout," as the pitcher was winding up on the mound? The greatest athletes in the world focus with one-pointed attention on success. On the occasions that this is not true, their performance suffers.

Unicycle

When I was nine years old, my father gave me a unicycle. It took me several weeks, but eventually, I learned to ride it. Over the years, I had lots of friends who wanted to learn to ride it. Most of them would hold onto a door frame as they mounted the unicycle. As soon as they let go of the support, the unicycle would fly off in one direction, and they in the opposite direction, landing flat on their backs.

Getting up from the floor, they would already be making excuses, blaming the unicycle, the carpet, or blaming me for not knowing how to teach. A few of my friends would push away from the door frame and fall just as fast and as hard, but they would jump up, exclaiming excitedly, "Did you see that!?" The more spectacular the wipe-out, the more excited they became. Guess which of my friends learned to ride the unicycle? When I asked myself what the difference was between those who quit and those who persevered, it was their goals.

When approaching any new skill that requires balance, most people choose the negative goal of not falling. For them, falling is a failure. Each fall leads to embarrassment and increasing frustration. Only a few people seem to focus on a version of the Blue Dot. As long as they stay focused on success, they do not see falling as a failure. That does not mean that they never fail. But each fall is another step on the path, bringing them ever closer to their Blue Dot of Success. Those friends who managed to stay in Flow, enjoying the process even while making mistakes, were the ones who persevered and eventually learned to ride the unicycle.

"To avoid situations in which you might make mistakes may be the biggest mistake of all." ~ Peter McWilliams

Mistakes are Feedback

In the Circle of Avoidance, success is vague (anywhere within the innermost circle is equally successful), but failure is precisely defined. By contrast, in the Blue Dot model, we see that success is clear and failure nonexistent.

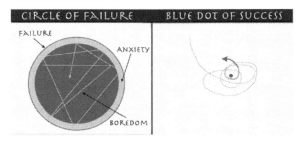

In the first model, we have sharp changes of direction to avoid failure, followed by periods of coasting in a straight line (anxiety followed by boredom). In the Blue Dot model, there are constant course corrections to be made, so you are never bored. Because failure does not exist in this model, there is no anxiety. What remains is Flow!

Look at what happens over time with these two models. When students approach balance poses by trying not to put their foot down, they start with big wobbles. As skill improves, they suppress those wobbles in smaller vibrations and eventually compressed rigidity.

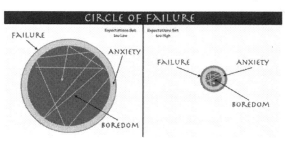

Long after they have learned not to fall, you still see the tension and anxiety in their faces, but never joy.

When your goal is positive, such as looking for relaxation and stillness in your balance poses, you have nothing to fear. You may put your foot down more often at first, but over time, skills improve. Your movements spiral toward that perfect balance, and you relax into stillness.

Now it is time to check back in with our straight-A student. Earlier, I said that wanting straight A's is usually a negative goal, but not always. Wherein lies the difference? Let's compare two classmates with the same goal of making straight A's this semester. The first student always makes straight A's every semester. Her goal is toxic. She has nothing to gain and everything to lose. She is bored when her grades are safe and anxious when her grades are in jeopardy.

The second student used to be a C student but has been working hard the past few years to raise her grades. She has never made straight A's in her life, but this semester, she has a shot. This student has nothing to lose and everything to gain! This student is chasing the Blue Dot of Success.

As you can see, the same goal can be toxic for one person while helping another student find Flow. The difference is a matter of perspective. One student is holding onto the past and defending the status quo; the other is busy creating a new future.

Growing up, my parents had different outlooks on life. Watching a bulldozer tear up a grass field, my mother was upset. She worried about the rabbits and other wildlife that lived in the field. She saw change as the destruction of what was.

My father, watching the same event, was delighted. "They are building a recreational center for at-risk-youth – indoor pool, tennis courts, the works!" he exclaimed triumphantly. My dad was always looking to the future. For him, change was an act of creation.

Between my parents, I realized that creation and destruction are flip sides of the same coin: transformation. In Buddhism, the first of the three Universal Truths is Annica - the recognition that everything is impermanent and changing. It is futile to resist change, and when we do, it leads to suffering.

Let's revisit the idea of expanding your Flow window. Most people either push into fear to escape from boredom or retreat into boredom to escape anxiety. Both strategies are negative; both are at-

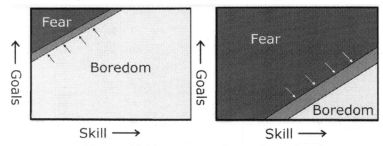

tempts at avoidance. Neither approach works and only serves to shift and constrict the Flow window. They are both negative goals and, therefore, toxic. As long as you hold onto the goal of avoiding either boredom or fear, you will never expand your Flow window.

Most people go through life trying and failing to avoid boredom and fear. Instead, choose to focus on a positive goal, the expansion of your Flow window. Along the way, be prepared to experience boredom and anxiety occasionally.

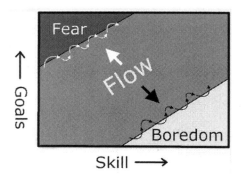

Now you have nothing to lose and everything to gain. To expand your Flow window, you must sometimes push into boredom and then turn around and push into fear to build a tolerance for both. The motivation of this action must be positive and in service to your Blue Dot.

I still find it fascinating to observe that those who seek to avoid boredom or fear end up experiencing more of both. In contrast, when you deliberately push into boredom and anxiety to expand your window of Flow, you end up living a life with less and less boredom and fear. Those seeking to expand Flow must view boredom and anxiety as opportunities to build resiliency in the face of both. So, how do we shift from a negative to a positive goal?

Step 1: Identify any goal based on avoiding failure or maintaining the status quo (even if it masquerades as a positive goal, like the student wanting to make straight A's, again).

Step 2: Choose a new, positive Blue Dot of Success. At this point, you must be especially cautious. Now that you have converted a 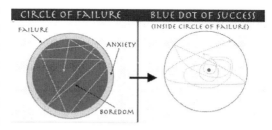 vague negative goal into a clear positive aspiration, it may be tempting to start chasing the new goal. But the Circle of Failure still lingers around the periphery. It may not simply disappear because you add a new goal. If you proceed to chase your Blue Dot before you erase any lingering Circle of Failure, you will generate the pattern at the far

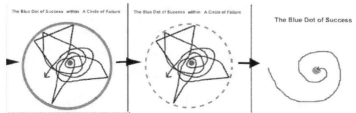

left in the diagram below.

When you are spiraling in on the Blue Dot, everything seems okay. But when you drift out toward the edge and the risk of failing, anxiety may trigger abrupt behavior changes to avoid perceived disappointment. Although you will have less boredom, anxiety will still be a problem.

Step 3: Erase attachment to the old, negative goal. This is often the hardest step to implement. We will consider this step in more detail momentarily.

Step 4: Pursue your new, positive goal.

Step 5: Respond to positive and negative feedback as you correct your trajectory and spiral in on success.

Some goals are more challenging to let go of than others. They are "sticky" - easier to pick up than to set aside. The goal of not putting your foot down in a balance pose is one such example. I have observed the same thing in hundreds of students taking my balance workshop.

Even after I explain positive and negative goals and ask them to let go of the negative goal of not putting their foot down, they still wobble and fight for control when they lose their balance.

To erase attachment to this negative goal, I often have students practice falling on purpose – but relaxing and breathing as they lose their balance and put their foot down. Then I put them in situations where I know they will lose their balance accidentally and challenge them to stay in Flow as they lose their balance. Gradually they learn how to stay relaxed and calm when they approach and cross what used to be a Circle of Failure.

Once they have erased the Circle of Failure from their consciousness, they are ready to focus on their Blue Dot of Success.

In martial arts, you practice falling until you are no longer scared to take a fall. In kayaking, you practice capsizing until you no longer fear losing your balance. Erasing the Circle of Failure by practicing "mistakes" can help you erase a stubborn toxic goal.

Of course, I would not recommend this approach when the cost of an error is too high.

Remember, when fully embracing the Blue Dot of Success, there is no failure. There is only feedback, which provides useful information to help you adjust your course as you zero in on success.

Revisiting Annica

Time is a peculiar phenomenon. Our experience of time changes with time. What seems like an eternity for a six-year-old child passes in a blink of the eye as we grow older. Time crawls when we are miserable and flies when we are in Flow.

Sometimes a fastball is a blur, and occasionally it seems to float, waiting for the batter to swing. But the one constant in all of this is: Time does not stop or move backward. It is when we resist the forward movement of time that we suffer. Buddha's great insight into reality: Annica (impermanence).

Imagine driving across a country. Looking ahead, you see landmarks: road signs, trees, windmills, two kids bouncing a ball, speed bumps on the road. These all lie ahead of you in the immediate future. As you pass each of these items, they move into your past.

There is no problem when a passenger turns their head to follow these sights out the back window. But if you are the driver, the very object that demanded your attention as you approached it, like the two kids bouncing their ball, becomes a dangerous distraction as you pass by. You might easily miss seeing the dog running across the road in front of you.

Because goals are rooted in the past and reach forward into the future, they are creatures of time. The future Flows into the present and the present into the past. There is no stopping or going back. Positive goals look forward and help shape the future.

Sooner or later, the future becomes the present, the present becomes the past, and you must release these old goals before they drag you into the past with them. Keep releasing old dreams and finding new goals as you live on the creative edge of time.

Tarzan

In the movies, Tarzan moves through the jungle canopy, swinging from vine to vine. As he reaches for the next vine, he releases the previous one. All forward movement relies on letting go of the past. This is critical to understand if you are to be the master of your own goals.

White Horse and Red Rose

At a conference I was attending, the keynote speaker instructed us to close our eyes and not think about a WHITE HORSE! I immediately thought about a white horse and heard scattered laughter around the auditorium from others who, like me, could not help themselves. If you try this exercise, you may discover that it is impossible. As soon as you try not to see the white horse, you become trapped in the Circle of Avoidance. Failure is clearly defined, but success is vague.

When I try this exercise with students, most readily admitted their failure. Occasionally, one or two might convince themselves that they succeeded. These are the students I am most interested in because I know that if they tried to avoid thinking about a white horse, they failed, whether they realize it or not. As they sit there, pleased with their success, I want to ask them why they are smiling. "Because

I am not thinking about a white horse!" they would have to reply. To avoid something, they have to know what it is they are trying to avoid. Part of their mind is watching the other part, saying to itself, "No white horses here!" This is a classic example of why negative goals fail.

Toward the end of the keynote, the speaker told us once again to close our eyes. "This time, I want you to see a red rose," he instructed. After a few minutes, he asked if anyone saw a white horse by mistake. Only two or three hands went up out of 800 people. Herein lies the difference between positive and negative goals.

Now that you know the secret to not thinking about white horses is to think about a red rose, you can use this trick yourself. The next time someone tells you not to think about a white horse, you will fill your mind with red roses (or chocolate ice cream). You might even think to yourself that this trick is working and start to smile. But if I were sitting next to you and asked why you were smiling, you would have to answer, "Because I am not thinking about white horses!"

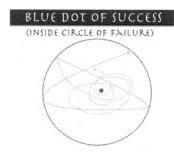

BLUE DOT OF SUCCESS
(INSIDE CIRCLE OF FAILURE)

Positive thinking fails when we use it to try and avoid negative thinking.

If the reason you were thinking about a red rose was to avoid thinking about a white horse, the red rose is secondary to the goal of avoiding the white horse. You will never escape the Circle of Failure in this manner. Once again, we can see how a negative goal manifests failure.

The Secret to Using Positive Goals

Steven hates anxiety and would rather be bored than anxious. Penelope hates being bored and would rather deal with anxiety. Both are motivated by the avoidance of that which they do not like.

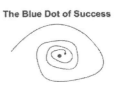

The Blue Dot of Success

The secret to using positive goals is to erase the Circle of Failure. In this case, it means that thinking about a white horse is not seen as failure or success. It is irrelevant. You focus on the red rose because it is your goal, not to avoid something else. If a white horse enters your mind, let it! Do not hold onto it. Do not push it away. Do not try to ignore it. Just gently return your attention to the red rose and let the white horse come and go. Eventually, the white horse will get bored and wander away, and you and your red rose will remain.

THE BLUE DOT OF SUCCESS + REMNANTS OF THE CIRCLE OF FAILURE = LINGERING ANXIETY

A Final Word on Balance

Balance is not about rigidity. It is not about control. When I balance kneeling on top of a therapy ball, I am not really in control; I am falling! Whatever direction I am falling in, I maneuver the therapy ball to keep it between me and the floor. You have probably already mastered this art of falling without ever hitting the ground. We call it walking! Stand still. Notice that before you can walk, you first must lean forward. As you start to fall, you swing a leg forward, keeping it between you and the floor. Before you walk backward, you first have to start falling back. Whatever direction you wish to walk in, you lean in that direction until you begin to fall and then manage to keep moving your legs to keep your feet under you as you are falling. It is the same with a unicycle. This is Flow. Falling without ever hitting the ground.

Now do the same thing with your life. A goal determines the direction you will fall. Then peddle as fast as your little legs can go to keep the unicycle under you. Let go and have fun! Make mistakes and learn from them. But remember, when making mistakes, don't be an idiot.

To learn from a mistake, you must first survive it. If you realize that you will not survive one of your mistakes, take comfort in the fact that others may learn from your example.

"If all else fails, immortality can always be assured by spectacular error." ~ John Kenneth Galbraith

Complimentary Models

Let's compare Mihaly Csikszentmihalyi's Flow model to the Blue Dot of Success. At first, they look quite different, but they actually complement each other. Both models help us to reduce boredom and anxiety and deepen Flow. Notice that in the Blue Dot, there are constant adjustments to the course. Similarly, the secret to staying in Flow in Mihaly's model is also continual adjustments to goals.

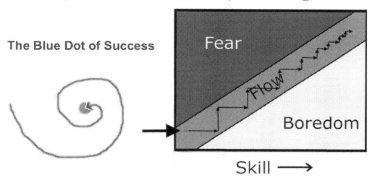

So why do we need both models, and how do they differ? The Blue Dot is most useful when looking at larger, long-term goals: vision, mission, and strategy. Flow is most useful in short-range goals: tactics and process.

Beginner's Luck

If you have played many board games, you may already be familiar with the expression, beginner's luck. I can't count how many times I have sat down with experienced players to learn a new game and won, much to their frustration. They often dismissed my accomplishments as mere 'beginner's luck.' Of course, subsequent games usually proved them right.

I have also been on the receiving end of this story. A few years ago, a friend and I decided to play a board game called Acquire. It is a strategy game, but there is also a small element of luck. We had played this game numerous times and considered ourselves experts. We needed a third player and convinced a mutual friend to give the game a try. We warned Amanda that it was a steep learning curve, and if she walked away without breaking the All-Time-Low-Score record, she could still hold her head high.

As expected, Amanda's play demonstrated a complete lack of understanding of the game and its complex and subtle strategies. But everything went her way, from the first play to the last. She was laughing and having a great time throughout it all. My friend and I tried to feel good for her, but it was difficult not to give in to mounting frustration as our luck evaporated.

Her play made no sense, and yet she won! My friend and I agreed that this was obviously a case of beginner's luck and immediately challenged her to a rematch! She declined our invitation and walked away undefeated, head held high and feeling very pleased with herself.

If we examine this phenomenon in terms of Flow, it will start to make more sense. Any casual observer of this game with Amanda would have noted that she was in Flow, and my gamer friend and I were not. The question is, why?

The first time someone plays a new game, they have no status quo to defend! They have less to lose and more to gain than the people teaching them. They are more likely to be operating within the blue-dot-of-success model than the circle of avoidance.

Although their skill level is very low, they are free to set their goals correspondingly low. For instance, they may not care about winning or losing. They might be focused entirely on learning and having fun. With the right goal, and by focusing their attention on that goal, they could easily achieve Flow. The deeper the Flow state, the 'luckier' we become! If this does not resonate with you, turn it around, and it might make more sense. Have you ever noticed how your luck gets worse and worse in lock-step with your mood?

We can divide learning into four levels:

1. Unconscious Incompetence.

2. Conscious Incompetence.

3. Conscious Competence.

4. Unconscious Competence.

As a beginner in any endeavor, you start at level one. This stage can be fun and is the source of what we call 'Beginner's Luck.'

Further growth requires that you move to level two, conscious incompetence. This level is frustrating because your goals are set higher, but your skills have not yet caught up. When you lose the Flow that you might have enjoyed at level one, your luck disappears as well. Often this results in a decline in your performance, leading to further frustration and less Flow. This is when you are most likely to give up and start looking for something else to do.

If you persevere, your skills will eventually catch up to the higher goals you have set for yourself, and you will reach level three, conscious competence. Here you may experience mild Flow states. Level three is a rewarding and satisfying stage, and it is now more likely that you will continue to work and improve.

As skill levels continue to improve, you may make it to level four, unconscious competence. This is where you look for deep Flow!

Stages one, three, and four are all pleasant. It is stage two that is frustrating and leads to so many people quitting a new activity. So, the question we need to ask is: what is the most effective way to move from stage two to stage three?

The most commonly used strategy is brute force. When people realize that progress is becoming more difficult, they keep their heads down and push harder. It requires a dogged determinism. It often does work, but it is exhausting, and it is slow going. The better approach is to try to stay in Flow while moving through level two.

From Chapter One, you may remember that the deeper your Flow, the faster your skills improve. Alternatively, the deeper the anxiety or boredom you are feeling, the slower skills improve. You may have already identified the secret to moving through stage two without losing Flow. First, break down the process into lots of smaller goals and arrange them logically like stepping stones from where you are to where you want to be. Then, and this is critical, forget about everything except for the next step you are about to take. If you have done a good job with choosing goals, each step, by the time you are ready to take it, should be challenging but not intimidating.

Falling from Grace

First, we need to revisit the idea of goals that may start healthy but later become toxic. Imagine Jordan, a young boy who dreams of becoming the boxing heavyweight champion of the world. He covers his bedroom walls with posters of his heroes. He is 11 years old, has nothing to lose and everything to gain; therefore, he is never bored or scared. This is a perfect example of the Blue Dot of Success.

When Jordan leaves his apartment building, he sees friends from school loitering on the street, selling drugs. He walks right by them on his way to the gym. The goal of becoming the heavyweight champion of the world is serving him well. There are many reasons he might lose interest in his dream as he grows older, and we have talked about those already in the chapter on Toxic Goals. But what happens if he does not lose interest? Suppose Jordan is 24 years old now, stands 5 feet 4 inches tall, and only weighs 117 pounds. He will never be a heavyweight boxer. What was a great goal at age 11 is now a toxic goal, and if he cannot let go of that dream, it will ruin the remainder of his life. But if he can let go of that old dream, he is free to pivot to a new goal, perhaps shooting for the world's bantamweight champion. There is no reason that his life cannot be just as focused on the new goal as the old, other than an inability to control his own goals. But if he still wishes, secretly, that he was a heavyweight? That unspoken lingering remnant of his original goal will undermine his new goal.

Suppose Jordan is 24 years old, stands 6 feet 2 inches tall, weighs 205 pounds, and has the reflexes of a tree sloth! He will never be any kind of boxing champion at any weight. Once again, a goal that served him well in the past is now toxic. But if he can let go of that goal, he is free to choose a new plan to regain Flow. Perhaps he will decide to open a boxing gym for at-risk youth in his old neighborhood.

It is not too much of a reach to imagine him at age 60, in his gym, surrounded by three generations of grateful students. He has seen the fate of more talented friends, who were destroyed by their success, and is feeling thankful for how his life turned out. But what if, when he opens his gym, there is a small part of him that still secretly wishes he had been a boxing champion? The kids will instinctively know that they are his second choice, which will undermine his new goal.

Finally, suppose that Jordan is 24 years old, stands 6 feet 2 inches tall, weighs 205 pounds, and has the reflexes of a mountain lion! He finally gets his shot at the heavyweight title. He has nothing to lose and everything to gain. In training, and on the night of the fight, he is in Deep Flow. Suppose he wins. What happens next?

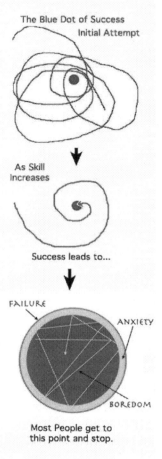

The Blue Dot of Success
Initial Attempt

As Skill Increases

Success leads to...

FAILURE

ANXIETY

BOREDOM

Most People get to this point and stop.

The next year, he accepts a challenge, and the promoter schedules another fight. During training, a reporter and cameraman show up at the gym for an interview. They stick a mic in his face and invariably ask some variation on the following question: "So, Champ, how does it feel to be defending your title?" I hate this question because it plants the idea of failure in the young athlete's mind.

His whole life, the goal of becoming the heavyweight champion has been the source of his Flow. But now, he has nothing to gain and everything to lose. Success is vague, and failure is clearly defined. His Blue Dot of Success has morphed into a Circle of Failure.

If the contender is really good, the champion knows fear for the first time in his life. If the contender is incompetent, the champ has to deal with boredom. In either case, there is no Flow. Whether the champion is dealing with boredom or fear, his training will suffer, as will his performance. Defending his title put him firmly within the Circle of Failure.

"In this world, there are only two tragedies. One is not getting what one wants, and the other is getting it. The last is much the worst; the last is a real tragedy!" ~ Oscar Wilde, Lady Windermere's Fan

Every goal becomes toxic at the moment of completion. It moves from the future to the past, becoming the new status quo! If you are not careful, you will transition from wanting to attain something to wanting to hold onto it.

The entire yoga system rests on two core principles: Abhyasa and Vairagya (practice and non-attachment). It is easy to pick up a shiny new marble. It is more challenging to recognize when it becomes toxic and release it. Even if you succeed temporarily, the toxic goal can sneak back in when you are not looking and take up residence, bringing with it boredom and fear. You must learn to notice when a toxic goal returns and erase it repeatedly until you are free from its influence.

Steven's Blue Dot of Success was to make a million dollars before he turned 25. In his pursuit of this goal, he had nothing to lose and everything to gain. Now Steven is 26 and is a millionaire. Without realizing it, his dream has morphed from wanting to make a million dollars into wanting to hold onto what he already has. This new goal will become the future source of boredom or fear. Steven has nothing to gain and everything to lose. His Blue Dot of Success has become a Circle of Failure. He will be anxious when his wealth is threatened and bored when it is not. This problem is all too common among the rich and powerful.

The concept of Vairagya (non-attachment) is Stephen's way out of this trap. He does not have to give all of his money to charity, but he must give away his psychological attachment to that money. If he succeeds in erasing this Circle of Failure, he can pursue a new Blue Dot of Success limited only by imagination.

For simplicity's sake, let's say that Stephen's new goal is to make two million dollars. If he has genuinely released all attachment to the one million dollars, then and only then will he have nothing to lose and everything to gain. He will be more likely to find his Flow state.

There is an old saying in business, "To make a second fortune, you must be willing to lose the first one." Easier said than done! It might help if Steven can remember that he wanted money in the first place to escape boredom and fear. Realizing that his attachment to money is the source of his boredom and fear, he might understand logically that this is a toxic goal and needs to be released. Seeing a trap is the first step in avoiding it.

It is not easy to give up psychological attachment to money, but it is possible. If Steven succeeds, he is one step closer to living a life beyond boredom and fear.

Once he has erased his Circle of Failure, all he needs is a new, challenging, and inspiring goal to chase after, whether making two million dollars or sailing around the world.

If you spend much time driving on country roads, you have probably come across more than a few dogs that love to chase cars.

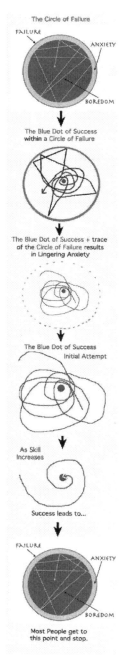

The Circle of Failure

The Blue Dot of Success
within a Circle of Failure

The Blue Dot of Success + trace
of the Circle of Failure results
in Lingering Anxiety

The Blue Dot of Success
Initial Attempt

As Skill
Increases

Success leads to...

Most People get to
this point and stop.

Even a dog is smart enough to know that if you catch the car, the game is over, and it is time to pursue a new goal. The joy is in the pursuit. Do not cling to a toxic goal. All goals become toxic at the moment of completion. We must let go of the past to embrace the future.

Let's rejoin our boxing champion. Jordan is 24 years old and the heavyweight champion of the world. He is surrounded by people who tell him he will soon be defending his title. Never let others tell you what your goal is. You must be free to choose your own goals. Defending your title is a toxic goal. You have nothing to gain and everything to lose. So how do you survive your success? How does Jordan regain his Flow?

He needs to find a new goal that accomplishes two things. It must first erase the Circle of Failure so that he has nothing to lose. Then he must challenge his current skill level to restore Flow.

Here is the first half of the new goal that I would suggest: "No matter whether I win or lose…" This portion erases the goal of defending his title, which society has prescribed, and frees him from the associated Circle of Failure. He is stating that he does not care about winning or losing anymore. Winning was yesterday's goal. For the second half of his statement, he needs to set an intention to regain his Flow. Considering that he is the heavyweight champion of the world, it is safe to assume that his skill level is already very high, so he needs to set the bar even higher to regain his Flow. Perhaps he might choose the following: "No matter whether I win or lose, I want this to be the fight of the century!"

If he genuinely does not care about winning or losing, he is fearless. If he wants this to be the fight of the century, he will not hold anything back from training. He has found his new Blue Dot of Success.

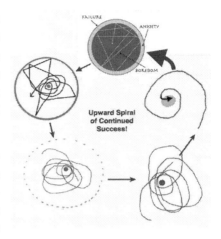

Upward Spiral
of Continued
Success!

During the months of training, he is smiling because he has a secret: He is not planning to defend anything! He is training to make history. He has nothing to lose and everything to gain. When the bell rings, he comes out of his corner in Deep Flow. Win or lose, people will be talking about this fight for a hundred years!

Notice that if Jordan wants to defend his title (he does not want to lose), he is more likely to be bored or scared in training and at the fight, and thus more likely to fail! When he permits himself to lose, sets his goal higher, and finds Flow, he is more likely to win!

If you are in the Circle of Failure (top of diagram), choose a new Blue Dot of Success. Then erase the Circle of Failure and spiral in toward the center of the Blue Dot. Once inside the Blue Dot, you will discover it has become the new Circle of Failure.

Around and around, you go. But with each cycle, you are also evolving, growing wiser, and more skilled in the use of goals to shape your life. So, the circle is actually an upward spiral of personal evolution. By constantly transforming our goals, we can maintain a continuity of Flow.

Ouroboros

In 1972, my father took me to see the Tutankhamun Exhibition at the British Museum in London. The treasures, dating from the 14th century BC, included a snake's image eating its tail, carved into the shrine surrounding the pharaoh's sarcophagus. This is the earliest known representation of the ouroboros.

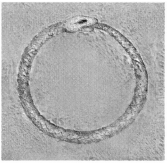

This ancient symbol of life has weathered three and a half millennia to remind us that continuity is only found through transformation.

At its heart is the ancient commandment, "Grow or die!" Or, as a friend once remarked during a nature documentary, "Eat and be eaten!" This is a fitting symbol for our final and perhaps most crucial insight into the Blue Dot of Success.

To rise above boredom and fear and experience continuity of Flow, you must learn to continually release your attachment to the past, live in the present, and look to the future. Those who resist change, and cling to the status quo, suffer at the hands of change.

Chapter Five

LIVING YOUR FLOW

In Demian, Herman Hesse writes, "Each man had only one genuine vocation — to find the way to himself... His task was to discover his own destiny — not an arbitrary one and live it out wholly and resolutely within himself. Everything else was only a would-be existence, an attempt at evasion, a flight back to the ideals of the masses, conformity, and fear of one's own inwardness."

Most people live out their lives like a dust mote caught in a ray of sunlight, dancing around randomly and subject to various currents and collisions. Some few, inspired by a higher calling, turn each current and every collision to their advantage to moving ever closer to realizing their vision. But first, they must identify this "higher calling" and then organize a set of goals to support them on their quest.

Hierarchy of Goals

For clarity, we can organize goals into the following categories by timespan: Vision, Mission, Strategic, Tactical, and Process. The most important of all goals is your vision. You

only have one goal at this highest level. All subsequent goals are in service to that vision. The timeline is infinite. This is a goal that we cannot complete. It is something to which we aspire.

Beneath the central vision, you need one or more specific mission goals. Mission goals directly support the vision and move you forward in that direction. The timeline for mission goals is long but finite. You hold them steady until completed and then discard them before they turn toxic.

For each mission goal, you will need to develop several strategic goals to support it. The timeline for strategic goals is moderate. Break each strategic goal down into several tactical goals or steps required to accomplish it. The timeframe for tactical goals is short. Finally, you can break tactical goals down into process goals.

Vision, mission, strategic and tactical goals are all about the future. Process goals live in the present moment. Use process goals to find, maintain, and maximize Flow. The timeline here is immediate. You must continually choose, and discard, process goals as needed to improve performance.

Celestial Navigation

"Do not be in a hurry to succeed. What would you have to live for afterward? Better make the horizon your goal; it will always be ahead of you." ~ William M. Thackeray

Traveling north, you will eventually arrive at a destination (the North Pole). From the North Pole, every direction is south. To continue your journey, you must first release the goal of traveling north. Only then are you free to choose a new destination. We look for this same quality in our mission, strategic, and tactical goals. They should all have clearly defined and achievable objectives that allow us to measure progress and know when we have arrived. Upon completion, they become toxic, and we should replace them to continue our journey. Traveling west is different. It is a direction, not a destination.

You can circle the planet endlessly and never arrive at "West." We look for this same quality in our vision goal.

Early sailors used the stars to help navigate and measure the progress of their voyage. Your vision goal serves a similar function in helping you navigate your life. It is the master goal that gives shape to the arc of your life. Just as the stars remain relatively constant over the centuries, your vision goal should remain consistent throughout your life.

When you are ready to start work on your vision, it is easier than you think!

I Know What You Want

Upon reflection, it might seem obvious that all people share some variation of the same vision, to live a life of Flow. We are hardwired to search for it. Revisiting the discussion of "Shadow Goals," you may already see the problem. We are motivated to want more Flow, but this can

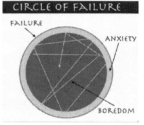

lead to an aversion for its opposite. Instead of actively seeking Flow, we try to avoid experiencing boredom and fear. When we seek to avoid boredom and fear, we diminish our tolerance for both. We become tangled in our own Circle of Failure.

On the other hand, if we focus on achieving more and deeper experiences of Flow utilizing the Blue Dot of Success model, we will see that experiencing boredom and fear helps expand our Flow window and leads to more and deeper Flow. So instead of avoiding boredom and fear, we turn them to our advantage.

We actively seek out boredom and fear but at a time and place of our choosing. And in beating them back, we expand our Flow window. As our Flow window opens, we end up having more profound Flow experiences, and incidentally, we experience less and less boredom and fear over time.

Once you realize this, you can take a firmer grasp on the reins of your life. Feel free to use "Living in Flow" for your vision, or find a similar sentiment (Love, God, Harmony, etc.) and state your vision in your own words. For instance, a yoga teacher might choose a vision of "Living my Yoga." A grandmother might choose a vision of "Sharing Flow with Family and Friends." When asked why he pursued what he called the theory of everything, the famous theoretical physicist Stephen Hawking replied, "to know the mind of God." This is a vision that demands Flow. There is no room for boredom or fear in such a quest.

Mission Goals: First Things First

Choosing and clarifying your mission goals is your next step. In his bestselling book, *The 7 Habits of Highly Effective People*, Stephen Covey's advice is to "Begin with the end in mind." Without a mission, you are wandering in the wilderness. Any progress you make in the meantime could easily turn out to be in the wrong direction.

Imagine that you adopt a dog suffering from separation anxiety. The next day, you get an offer to spend three months traveling in Asia, writing for a magazine about your experiences. You realize that being a travel writer is what you genuinely want to do with the next part of your life. This is your Flow. Now you have two competing and conflicting goals. If you turn down the job offer to spend time with your dog during this critical adjustment period, there is a possibility that in some small way, you might grow to resent the dog you rescued. If you push your dog off on a friend (a very good friend), you might find yourself feeling guilty and unable to enjoy the writing and travel as much as you hoped. The sooner you clarify your mission-level goals, the sooner you can organize the rest of your life to avoid similar problems.

Stepping Stones

Once you have your vision and one or more mission goals, you are ready to organize your supporting goals. At the top of your vision board, put your vision (some variation on living in Flow). Beneath your vision, fill in one or more mission-level goals.

Break down the most immediate mission goal into several strategic goals. Take the first strategic goal and break it down into several tactical goals. These are laid out like stepping stones to create a path from the present moment toward your mission.

Examine every step to see if it distracts from or actively sabotages any of the more critical goals above it, all the way up the hierarchy to the top-level vision. To the degree that it does, consider discarding it in favor of a better goal. Often, we suffer not from too few goals but too many. Extraneous goals diffuse our energy to the point that we become immobilized. Remove the cobwebs of old and distracting dreams, then double down on what remains – the plans you are truly passionate about that support your highest aspirations.

If you find resistance to eliminating a distracting goal, remind yourself that you can always pick up the discarded goal and resume work on it after accomplishing your current mission.

The Blue Dot of Success model is critical in choosing your long-range goals of Vision, Mission, and Strategy. As you shift toward more immediate goals, the tactical and process goals,

Blue Dot of Success

Vision

Mission

Strategy

Tactics

Performance

Deep Flow

110

the Flow model dominates. The Blue Dot model helps you choose your target, and the Flow model helps you get there.

You do not need to fill in the entire vision board with details down to the tactical level. It is enough to have at least one mission and the strategies to support it. Then take the most immediate strategy and fill in the tactics to support it.

There is no real need to enter process goals because they are constantly updated, on the fly, in response to real-time feedback.

"God made the world round so we would never be able to see too far down the road." ~ Isak Dinesen

Fixed Destination, Flexible Route

Your mission goal needs to be stable, only changing when it conflicts with your vision goal. The rest of your goals are increasingly more flexible as you go down the scale from strategic goals toward process goals. As circumstances change, you update your path and choose new strategic, tactical, and process goals to accomplish your mission goal. While sharing a common destination of the ocean, each drop of rain remains fluid, navigating a unique path through the terrain.

Imagine you have decided to vacation in Venice. You know where you are now (present moment). You know where you are going (Venice). Everything in between is negotiable and subject to change as needed. For instance, if you intended to travel by train from Paris to Venice, a rail strike could force you to pivot to a new strategy. Holding onto the destination while being flexible about the path increases the odds of success.

If Venice turns out to be closed to visitors (not so hard to imagine in a post-COVID-19 world), this goal may become toxic. If this happens, take a moment to revisit your hierarchy of objectives. Imagine, for instance, that your vision goal is to lead an adventurous life, and your mission goal is to travel to unique destinations on every continent. Your strategic goal is to visit Venice. Hold onto your vision and mission goals, and choose a new strategic goal that is not toxic, like visiting Florence, Naples, or Transylvania.

How often does a bump in the road unnecessarily ruin a vacation? When we lose sight of what is truly important to us, to pursue the more immediate strategic and tactical goals, tragedy ensues. On the other hand, if you can hold tightly to your higher-order goals while adjusting your lower-order goals to stay in Flow, you will enjoy the journey no matter what obstacles life throws in your path. The worst destination experienced in Flow is better than the best destination experienced while bored or scared.

"Be like water making its way through cracks. Do not be assertive, but adjust to the object, and you shall find a way around or through it." ~ Bruce Lee

Priming the Pump

When I was eight, my mother took me along on a visit to a college friend who had married a rancher. They lived on several thousand acres in South Texas. Her husband gave me a tour of the property while his wife and my mother visited. Although they had modern plumbing, they still had an old-fashioned water pump behind the kitchen. He invited me to pump the handle, but no water came. He then gave me a bucket of water from beside the pump, green with algae. He told me to pour it into the opening at the top of the pump. He explained that the water would displace the trapped air in the pipe, and only then would the pump be primed. This time, when I pumped the handle, water started to gush out onto the ground with each stroke. At first, it was the same green water I had poured into the pump, but soon it started to run clear and fresh. As I pumped, he refilled the bucket and left it beside the pump.

This experience of priming a pump was so common one hundred years ago that the federal government used the expression to explain their fiscal policy to the U.S. population. It is still commonly used to describe a situation where you first have to invest before getting a greater return.

The advertising industry makes use of this principle. They spend money to push ideas deep into your subconscious mind in the hopes that this will alter future behavior, i.e., more consumers purchasing their brand. How many times do they show the same ad? There is a reason for this repetition. The brain is all too quick to forget information that is not important. Something that you pay attention to several times a day for days, weeks, or months must be very important!

You can use this same force for good! You can prime your own pump to influence your future behavior toward your goal. If you can pay a little attention to your mission goal several times a day, you can begin to program your mind for future success.

One of the most effective ways to keep your mission front and center is to create a mission board. This is displayed where you will see it occasionally during the day. It helps you keep your project in mind. It enables you to track your progress. Most importantly, it primes the pump. By looking at your mission board at least once a day, you remind the subconscious mind that this is important to you.

Here is an example of how this works. This morning, I woke up remembering a dream about my earliest experiences with the internet. The Netscape browser was released in 1994. A whole new world opened up to me. My first great find was a free video game out of

Germany that I downloaded and played obsessively for several weeks. It consisted of a conveyor belt carrying assorted sizes and shapes of pipe. Unused pipes fell off the end of the conveyor, and after the third pipe fell, the game ended. Using a mouse to pick up and carry pieces of pipe and the keyboard to rotate them, you tried to fix a plumbing leak and connect the water mains to an apartment building. If you succeeded, a half-naked woman would lean out the window and say, "thank you!" in German. It was a stupid game, but everything on the internet was still new and exciting. The idea of reaching halfway across the world in the middle of the night, and downloading free software, was right out of science fiction.

Meanwhile, two friends were playing a computer game called Warcraft: Orcs and Humans. They played almost every evening and late into the night. After several weeks they stopped playing the game. I asked why they had stopped, and they sheepishly confessed that they had both started dreaming at night about Warcraft.

I teased them for a few days until I had my own nightmare. Instead of leading great armies to battle against hordes of orcs, I found myself surrounded by conveyor belts trying to fix leaking plumbing fixtures. I quit the video game the next day.

I had not thought about those two video games in twenty years. So why did I wake up on this particular morning thinking about them? Because I had spent a lot of time the previous evening researching priming pumps in preparation for writing this chapter. The last thing I did before going to bed that night was to look for images of old-fashioned water pumps. During the night, my subconscious mind went to work on the problem. The next morning, I remembered these two examples of how playing video games can affect dreams. Mission boards work similarly to move information into the subconscious mind.

Keep your vision, mission, and strategies front and center. As the subconscious mind realizes that this is important to you, it will work on your behalf. The more emotion or passion you feel, the harder the subconscious mind will work on your behalf. On the other hand, you are always free to keep playing video games during the day and dream about playing video games at night.

There is another positive effect of enlisting your subconscious mind in service to your mission goals. You may start to notice more coincidences and synchronicities in the real world that move you forward toward your strategy and mission goals, often in unexpected ways. One explanation is that your subconscious mind reprograms its filters to allow pertinent information to come to your attention that it usually would filter out.

Some people prefer supernatural explanations to explain these coincidences. Having experienced a few synchronicities that defied logical explanation, I understand this allure. Regardless of which explanation you subscribe to, most agree that the technique often works amazingly well.

Advertisers know that emotion helps plant stronger memories in the brain. Moreover, people act from emotion more consistently than from logic. Advertisers are masters of emotional manipulation. They use images, music, and stories to try to invoke emotional reactions.

Take back control of this powerful tool, and use it to enlist your subconscious mind in the service of your mission. You need to create a mission board that invokes an emotional response when you look at it.

Imagine a 16-year-old high school junior, Jennifer, whose mission is to become a marine biologist. Notice that the first mission board is just words and has a sparse emotional impact on the observer. To help engage your mind emotionally, use two or more vibrant colors in your mission board.

Words are okay, but for heavy lifting, colorful pictures work better. When Jennifer adds one or more striking images to her mission board, she gets an even stronger emotional response. When she couples a great picture with a logical, organized, and well-thought-out action plan, she maximizes her chances for success.

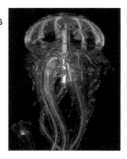

Every time Jennifer enters or leaves her bedroom, she sees this mission board. She is constantly reminding herself, both her conscious and unconscious mind, of what her priorities are in life.

The following mission board is for a couple who are just starting to plan their retirement.

Notice how the image is more likely to evoke an emotional response than just words and arrows. It is this more robust, emotional response that helps prime the pump. The image reinforces the importance of the other information on the board with the subconscious mind.

Assuming that your mission is important to you, it makes sense to maximize your odds for success. Consider using music to support the image's emotional content, while words and arrows carry the logical content. Once you have your mission in mind, find the right image and add it to your board. Then looking at the image, and thinking about the mission, identify the emotion that this evokes. Identify movies that create this emotion and listen to the soundtrack.

Imagine that Jennifer was inspired to become a marine biologist by the BBC documentary, Blue Planet. Now she looks at her favorite images of jellyfish, studies her mission board, and listens to the soundtrack of Blue Planet. In this way, she is maximizing her emotional engagement as she plans out her strategies and tactics.

Imagine looking at the couple's image on the beach while listening to "The Promise" soundtrack by Michael Nyman from the 1993 movie, The Piano. With sufficient repetition, this mission goal will take up residence in your mind along with the strategies and tactics.

The goal will become increasingly important to your subconscious, which in turn will go to work, removing obstacles that block your path. Joseph Campbell was fond of saying, "Follow your bliss, and doors will open, where before there were no doors."

Dharana: Deep Flow

For goals to work well, we must master them at every level. Performance without vision is the worst form of drudgery. Vision without performance is merely a daydream. The real magic happens when you have a vision, create a road map to actualize that vision, and then perform well along the way.

Having a mission and supporting strategies and tactics is critical to your success, but do not dwell on them. They are all rooted in the future. They distract you from the present moment, which is where all progress is made or lost!

Once you have a clear path laid out in your mind or on a mission board, keep your focus on its execution. Use process goals to help you concentrate with one-pointed attention. The deeper your focus, the more satisfying the experience will be, and the better you will perform. Deep Flow is both the means and the ends. This state of focused attention is what yoga refers to as dharana, the sixth limb of yoga.

From Csikszentmihalyi's work on Flow, we learned that the secret to performing well turns out to be goals! If goals are set too low, we become bored and make mistakes. If goals are set too high, we become nervous and make mistakes.

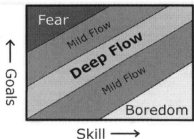

When we learn to choose appropriate goals, we can minimize boredom and anxiety and increase our peak experiences' duration and intensity. In doing so, we also improve performance. But that is only part of the solution. It is not enough to have the right goal; we still have to apply ourselves to that goal.

If you attempt to focus on this moment to achieve a future goal, it does not work. There is an inherent flaw in this strategy - the part of you thinking about the future. No matter how small that part is, it will distract you from your present moment performance. You will never experience Deep Flow as long as any part of you is focused on a future reward; Flow must be its own reward.

In dharana, there is no past, no future, only the eternal now. Pay attention to this moment for the present moment experience of paying attention. If you have never experienced Deep Flow, this may not make much sense to you yet. For those who have, you already know that Deep Flow has always been the goal.

"Nobody trips over mountains. It is the small pebble that causes you to stumble. Pass all the pebbles in your path, and you will find you have crossed the mountain." ~ Ralph Waldo Emerson

It is not a great mystery. Either we choose to pay attention, or we don't. Imagine washing the dishes. If your goal is in the future (to finish the dishes), you will probably be a little bored while doing them, maybe a little careless, and certainly not in Deep Flow. Now, imagine how you would wash a newborn baby's face for the first time. How much awareness? How light your touch? If someone gave you a baby right now to look after, could you choose to pay that much attention? If the answer is yes, then you will recognize that paying attention is a choice.

A newborn baby needs your attention, so you choose to give it. On the other hand, the dishes do not require anything from you. You must choose to pay attention for the sake of paying attention. Can you focus with one-pointed attention on washing the dishes and sustain that level of pure concentration for five minutes? This is how we cross the mountain… one pebble at a time. Like any muscle, your powers of concentration and willpower will grow stronger with exercise.

Deep Flow (or dharana) is a state of pure concentration, where duality collapses, and you become one with the object of your attention. You cannot find Deep Flow; if you are lucky, Deep Flow will find you. This is axiomatic. Deep Flow arises from a perfect acceptance of and merging with the reality of the present moment. Looking for something implies dissatisfaction with the present moment. So, the search for Deep Flow prevents Deep Flow!

Does this mean that we do not search for Flow? No, not at all! Here is where we need to distinguish between the various levels and functions of goals. At the level of vision, wanting to experience Deep

Flow increases the likelihood that you will. Likewise, mission, strategic, and tactical goals (such as deciding to read this book or practice meditation) can also increase the possibility of experiencing Deep Flow. But at the level of process goals, where Deep Flow resides, there is no technique. All of the preparations arise from the desire to experience dharana. But dharana occurs when we let go of desire and embrace what is.

"Meditation is one of the greatest arts in life — perhaps the greatest, and one cannot possibly learn it from anybody, that is the beauty of it. It has no technique and therefore no authority." ~J. Krishnamurti

Create an environment conducive to Flow, concentrate on what you are doing, and enjoy the present moment experience. We practice Flow, and occasionally, if we are lucky, Deep Flow finds us.

The Warrior's Path

When walking cross country: Spend 5% of the time looking back, lest you forget who you are and where you come from; 5% of the time looking to the horizon, lest you wander aimlessly and never arrive at your destination; and 90% of the time, watching where you step.

Keep track of your successes, failures, and lessons learned along the way, and occasionally take a moment to review your progress. Examining your past helps you understand who you are in the present, measure your progress, and feel the momentum that carries you into the future. It allows you to identify past mistakes and learn from them. The more you understand how your habits shape your life, the more empowered you are to make different choices, more aligned with the future you hope to create.

Furthermore, to release attachments to the past that prevent you from moving forward, you must see and understand what you are removing. The trick, when examining your history, is not to get trapped there. Look back not to wallow, but to understand the present moment and shape the future.

Looking to the future is essential if you want to participate consciously in its creation. While doing this, you will need to use creativity (associated with slower alpha and theta brainwaves) and critical thinking and problem solving (associated with faster beta brainwaves). It is relatively easy to speed brainwaves up but challenging to slow them down.

You can verify this for yourself by timing how long it takes you to go from worrying to relaxation and compare that to how fast you can go from relaxation to worrying. With this information in mind, organize your time to support creative work before engaging in critical thinking and problem-solving.

Before checking your cellphone in the morning, your brainwaves are more likely to be in the alpha or theta range. After a yoga class, massage, or meditation, you may also notice your brainwaves are slower and more conducive to creativity. Use these moments to prime the pump. While in this relaxed mental state, take a moment to daydream about how it will feel when you complete a current mission goal. It does not have to take a lot of time. Thirty seconds is sufficient. The key is repetition – once or twice a day is ideal. With each repetition, you are emphasizing the importance of this goal to your subconscious mind.

Later in the day, when your brain is in a beta frequency, take a few minutes to engage in critical thinking and problem-solving. Is your current plan still the best path from where you are to where you want to be? Review your mission board with a critical eye to identify what is working and change that which is not. Pay particular attention to tactical goals, which are more immediate and transitory.

In addition to the daily check-in with your goals, it is crucial to do a deeper dive several times a year or anytime you complete a mission goal. This process will take more time, at least an hour (some people take a day or weekend), and require that you be deeply relaxed and undistracted. You may find it helpful to get away from home for this step. A retreat or vacation may free you from household distractions.

Yoga or a massage can help set the stage for you to be in the right mood.

Begin by reviewing your vision goal. Daydream about new and different ways you might better accomplish your vision. At this stage, do not worry about practicalities; just let your mind run wild. Next, ask yourself if your current goals are serving you well or if they need to be adjusted or replaced.

Finally, as your brain is returning to critical thinking and problem-solving mode, consider all of the ideas you encountered when daydreaming. Decide whether you need to adjust, replace or eliminate any of your current mission goals. Finally, time permitting, examine each mission goal to see if the strategic goals that support it need to be adjusted.

The most challenging aspect of the warrior's path is spending 90% of the time watching where you put your foot down. Practice will help you develop this skill. Start by practicing dharana, the yoga art of concentration, for five minutes every day. Choose something as a target, and see if you can achieve one-pointed attention. Do not grip this attention, but rather hold it softly.

Remember the white horse and the red rose? Do not try to avoid distractions. Instead, gently bring your attention back to the target, again and again. You can focus on your breath, on washing dishes, on driving to work. Whatever you choose as a target, measure progress by the quality and duration of your attention. As this becomes easier, try ten minutes of concentration for its own sake. Then try doing this two or three times a day. Over time, you will be able to pay more attention to life with less effort. Concentration becomes a habit!

When you are not performing well, recognize whether you suffer from apathy or anxiety. Then identify the responsible goal and erase it. Finally, choose a new objective to return to a Flow state. This process is ongoing, taking place on a timescale of seconds and minutes.

Rising Above Boredom

Imagine you have to wash the dishes. If you do not choose your goal deliberately, your subconscious mind will provide one for you. In this case, it may well be "to finish washing the dishes."

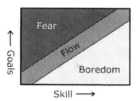

For most people, this is a toxic goal that will result in boredom. If you have washed dishes before, your skill level is probably high. So from the Flow model, we can see that the goal of finishing the dishes is set too low and will result in boredom.

Moreover, you have more to lose than to gain! Finishing the dishes will not make you feel incredibly proud or accomplished. However, failing to complete them will most likely leave you feeling deflated. Your focus, therefore, will be on avoiding failure rather than on achieving success. You are operating in the Circle of Failure.

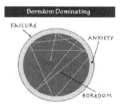

The goal of finishing the dishes is not objectively toxic; it is subjective. Imagine someone who has never washed dishes. We can safely assume that their skill level for washing dishes is lower, so the goal of finishing the dishes could be sufficiently challenging for them to be in Flow! Moreover, they have less to lose and more to gain, so their focus naturally gravitates toward achieving success, not avoiding failure. They may very well be following the Blue Dot of Success.

A very wealthy student attended a yoga retreat with me at an isolated retreat center. It was the first time in his life that he had gone anywhere without bodyguards. On the fifth day of the retreat, he went through the dining room as we were finishing dinner, cleaning off the tables, and carrying dirty dishes to the kitchen. He had never bussed a table in his life and was grinning from ear to ear! Boredom does not reside in any activity but in what we bring with us to the undertaking.

Rather than focus on whether or not you will finish washing the dishes, choose a specific goal that is positive and challenging. You could try to wash the dishes while balancing on one leg. You could time yourself with a stopwatch to see how fast you can clean the dishes while still doing a good job. The next day, try to beat your original time. You could try closing your eyes, focusing on the sounds, or feeling the dishes and water. You could practice qigong while washing dishes. You could practice pranayama (breath control) by trying to wash the dishes before you have taken ten breaths of air. There is an infinite number of goals to choose from: some boring, some scary, and some that will help you find Flow.

View repetitive activities as an opportunity to build a tolerance for boredom, a challenge to overcome by finding Flow. Keep bringing your attention to the process, especially to the senses (sight, sound, smell, touch, etc.). When writing, focus on the sensation of your pen gliding across the page, your wrist's movement, or the rhythmic sound of fingers striking keys. Find pleasure in the doing, and you will be in the zone. As you move along the path you sketched out on your mission board, take larger and more frequent steps. When bored, add challenging deadlines.

Reviewing your mission goal is another trick to offset boredom. Imagine how it will feel to complete this mission. Remember that the rewards of succeeding will justify the effort required to push through this temporary resistance. If this does not work for you, it may mean that you need a better mission goal that inspires greater commitment.

"Dream no small dreams for they have no power to move the hearts of men." ~ Johann Wolfgang von Goethe

Most importantly, blaming your internal state of mind on your circumstances is a fast track to learned helplessness. People who are fun bring the fun with them! If you are bored, it is because you are boring! But you can change. Choose to exercise your fun. Look for Flow in all areas of your life. In time, you will get better at finding it.

Tackling Fear

Figure out the source of your anxiety. Are you looking to the distant future? Or is it a present-moment crisis? If contemplating your mission or strategic goals is making you anxious, look at your mission board. See the stepping stones laid out from where you are to the completion of the mission. Either trust the path you have created, or create a new approach that you can trust. Then look at where you are putting your foot down. Nine times out of ten, if you believe in the path and only look one small step ahead, you can find your Flow.

If the anxiety is more immediate and revolves around the next step you are about to take, break it down into two or three smaller steps. Focus solely on the first of those. If anxious, consider moving more slowly along your path or even backtracking to a process goal that was a little more comfortable. Sooner or later, you will get bored, and it will be time to try the more advanced goal again. Sometimes just giving yourself an extension, or eliminating a deadline, can reduce the distress (and sometimes, in the absence of the anxiety, you end up in Deep Flow and make the deadline anyway).

Imagine you are anxious about giving an upcoming speech in front of 500 colleagues. If you look at this from a Flow perspective, your expectations exceed your skill. You may also be trapped in the Circle of Failure model, hoping you do not freeze up on stage. A negative goal with overly-high expectations will always result in anxiety. Erase the old goal, and replace it with a specific intention that is positive and challenging but not intimidating.

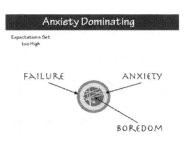

If your original goal was to give a fantastic speech that everyone would love, replace it with something better suited to your low skill level. Choose goals such as showing up on time and not leaving the stage before you have finished, no matter how difficult it is. If you accomplish these new goals, consider it a success, and prepare to take the next step on your journey. Remember, lower the bar enough, and the fear will fall away.

If your goal has placed you in a Circle of Failure, identify what you do not want to happen. For example, you may be worried that you will freeze on stage. Recognize that trying not to fail is the surest path to failure, and then erase the Circle of Failure. One way to do this is to ask what the worst-case scenario is. Look at it head-on. Imagine it happening. See a path through the worst-case scenario, and know that you can survive even this. Take a moment to think about what good could come out of such a trial (for instance, you could imagine yourself more resilient and fearless on the other side of such a test).

You are not saying that you want to fail, only that if you fail, it is not the end of the world. From the future, looking back, you might very well see that such a failure played an important part in your journey to eventual success.

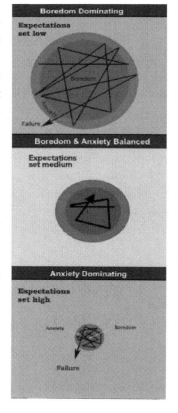

When Boredom & Fear Conspire

Sometimes we experience boredom and anxiety simultaneously. Often this is the result of setting a negative goal that is vague and insufficiently challenging. When we choose a negative goal but fail to clearly define what constitutes failure, we can simultaneously suffer from boredom and anxiety. Because we do not have a clear idea of success, we are bored and drift. Because we do not have a clear understanding of failure, we can never be sure that we are not about to fail. The solution is to identify the vague, negative goal and replace it with a positive, specific objective.

Sometimes the problem is that you are splitting your attention between a long-range mission or strategic goal that is causing the anxiety and the immediate process goal responsible for your boredom. Imagine that you are studying to become a surgeon. This goal seems so far beyond your present skill level that it makes you anxious. Simultaneously, you are bored memorizing the names of the bones in the human wrist. Eliminate the anxiety by creating a clear road map comprised of strategic and tactical goals arranged in small, achievable steps. Then direct your full attention to the present moment. Eliminate the boredom by creating better process goals and rewards. For instance, you could give yourself ten minutes (with a stopwatch) to memorize five bones and set a prize of ordering out your favorite pizza - but only if you are successful.

The Flow model can explain another reason for feeling boredom and fear simultaneously. If you have a big jump between two process goals, you can easily get stuck. The first goal is boring, so you fail to pay attention. The second goal is scary, and you learn nothing. After bouncing back and forth between boredom and fear with little progress, you end up quitting.

Remember that between boredom and fear, there is always a window of Flow. The secret to finding Flow is to create one or two smaller steps to bridge the larger gap between your two original goals. Choose the first of these smaller steps and focus until you find Flow. As your skill improves, take another small step, and before you know it, you are on the other side of the great divide, moving on down the road to success.

Specificity of Goals

In previous chapters comparing the Circle of Failure to the Blue Dot of Success, we already noticed that a clear and specific goal (Blue Dot) is more powerful and motivating than a vaguely defined idea of success. The fact is, vague and fuzzy goals give vague, fuzzy feedback. Specific goals provide specific feedback, which is essential to growing, learning, and improving. The children's parlor game of "Hotter/Colder" is a prime example of learning from feedback. In this game, one person leaves the room while their friends choose an object or hide something. When the person re-enters the room, they have to find the mystery object without talking. Their friends can only guide them by saying "Hotter" or "Colder," depending upon whether they are moving closer or further away from the object.

So why set vague goals? If the goal is sufficiently nebulous, you do not have to worry about failing. Instead of trying to throw a basketball through a small hoop, designate the bleachers as your target, and you can't miss! But now, your target is so big that every throw is equally good (I hit the bleachers yet again), so there is no discernment and thus no improvement in skill. Secondly, it's boring. This is why basketball is more popular than "bleacher ball." As long as we value not making mistakes more than we love growth, learning will stagnate.

When I was working in a hospital pharmacy and hating my job, I developed a habit of being right on time or a little late. When confronted about this pattern by a supervisor, I knew they were right and promised to try and do better in the future. Looking back, this was a pathetic goal that did nothing to help my performance or attitude at work. You can almost hear the learned helplessness in my voice.

Why was this such an ineffective goal? First, it is so vague that success and failure are difficult to establish. Better than what? Better at what? What is the timeline? Sometime in the future? When will I know if I succeeded or failed? And don't get me started on the word "try." This goal is an excuse for continued mediocrity. I can always fall back on, "Well, I tried."

Compare the previous goal to the following: "I promise to be early or on time for work every single day this next week." I can measure and quantify this goal. Is there a potential for failure? Yes. But if I miss the mark, I will know it. I can pick myself up, recalibrate, and make sure I get it right next time. In the attempt to hit the Blue Dot, you spiral toward the center, and performance will improve even if you do not hit the dot your first time.

The more precise the target, the better the feedback, and the more you learn. Remember, the great danger for those who continue to focus on not failing is that they will make the target so large, they can hit it without aiming. Then they get bored and careless, and manage to miss it anyway!

Commitment to Goals

Julian the Apostate, Emperor of Rome, invaded Persia in 363 AD. After his army successfully crossed the Tigris River, he burned all of the boats and pontoons behind them, thus ending the possibility of retreat. Every soldier knew their lives now depended upon going forward, no matter the hardship or perils they faced.

Burning the bridge instilled a clarity of purpose; like it or not, they were committed. This strategy goes in the face of the modern-day warning, "Don't burn your bridges," meaning keep your options open. Commitment collapses possibilities in favor of one chosen path forward. By eliminating distractions, it helps us to focus. Success is more likely, but failure is more painful.

When you commit, your self-worth is at stake! Promises kept increase self-worth. Broken obligations destroy self-worth. Have you ever heard someone at a New Year's Eve party announce that they would quit smoking? If this is the third time they have made such a commitment in the past three years, everyone rolls their eyes. Even the person committing does not believe it. It is more of a prayer than a promise.

Commitments are powerful tools when used well but dangerous when misused. Therefore, never make commitments carelessly. Use commitments sparingly, but to good effect, and to see them through.

To summarize, commitments are: specific and positive (Blue Dot), achievable (Flow), finite (shorter timelines tend to work better), and sacred.

Let me share one example of the power of committing oneself to a goal. In August of 1997, I relaxed at my favorite bakery with a coffee cup when a young man asked if he could sit at my table. Without looking up from the conference brochure I was studying, I nodded my head.

I could feel him watching me intently. I finally lowered the brochure and looked up. He then announced that he was organizing a conference. He seemed far too young to be planning a conference, but I asked him what his conference was about, just to be polite. "Integrating spiritual values into the workplace," he replied without missing a beat. Now he had my attention.

I taught yoga, meditation, and stress management for 3M, Apple, Motorola, and IBM. I had just presented at a national wellness conference on self-transformation to an audience primarily comprised of corporate human resource managers.

I put down the brochure and gave him my full attention. Kyle turned out to be an undergraduate student at the University of Texas School of Business. I asked him if he had any sponsors for his conference. No. I asked him if he had any speakers lined up. No.

People with big plans are a dime a dozen, and I was just about to disengage and resume reading my brochure when I asked one last question. "So, what have you done?" He looked me straight in the eye and said, "I put down $2,000 of my own money as a deposit with the Austin Convention Center for the weekend of May 7-9, 1998."

His first act was to commit himself personally to his vision. The effect this had on me was profound. I realized that there was no way he could pull this off without a lot of help. I also knew that I had all of the contacts he would need to help make this happen. By the end of the week, I was his business partner.

Due in large part to Kyle's commitment to his vision, more people started volunteering to help. No one wanted to see him fail. Neither Kyle nor I had any experience in event planning, and neither of us was detail-oriented. The next nine months were the most stressful of my life. Three months out from the conference, I suffered from nausea, headaches, insomnia, and visibly graying hair at the temples.

Eventually, I realized that Kyle was committed, but I was entertaining the idea of canceling the conference and refunding the sponsors' money. I was stuck sitting on the fence, and my fear was contagious. Fewer and fewer volunteers showed up to our work meetings, and no one wanted to invest more money in a sinking ship.

I looked hard at the worst-case scenario, imagining what would happen if we went ahead with the conference and everything went wrong. I realized that as painful as it might be, I could survive such a failure. I took a deep breath and set aside all thoughts of turning back. Full steam ahead, come rain or shine!

My fear receded, and confidence returned. Now sponsors started to return my calls. Once Kyle and I found our Flow, we started having fun with the work. Old volunteers returned, and new ones followed. In the last week running up to the conference, many of our volunteers started reporting their own profound Flow experiences. In the end, the conference was a resounding success, and even made a profit of two thousand dollars.

When I calculated my hourly income for the year that I worked on the event, it came to about 50 cents an hour. But the fact that we did not lose money was a miracle, and I still look back to that year as one of the most profound of my life.

In summary, it was Kyle's commitment that launched the conference, and eventually, my commitment that helped get it over the finish line.

"Nothing in this world can take the place of persistence. Talent will not; nothing is more common than unsuccessful people with talent. Genius will not; unrewarded genius is almost a proverb. Education will not; the world is full of educated derelicts. Persistence and determination alone are omnipotent. The slogan' press on' has solved and always will solve the problems of the human race." ~ Calvin Coolidge

It's Just a Matter of Time

"To achieve great things, two things are needed: a plan, and not quite enough time." ~ Leonard Bernstein

Time does not apply to vision goals because they are permanent, and their timeline is infinite. At the other end of the spectrum, time does not affect process goals because they are transient, and their timeline is immediate. In between, when working with mission, strategic, and to a lesser extent, tactical goals, timelines are critical.

A timeline makes the goal feel more real, which helps to prime the pump. Deadlines are an effective strategy to ward off procrastination and prevent boredom. In the mission goal examples earlier, the couple planning their retirement specified the date they planned to move to the Caribbean. This specificity does two things right off the bat. It puts pressure on the couple to start preparations now, and it also makes the goal seem more tangible. Seeing the date says to the subconscious mind, "This is going to happen!" Another advantage is that, over time, you can see if you are ahead or falling behind schedule.

The timeline is a tool that you use to help manifest your mission and vision. Do not become a slave to a timetable. Hold to it as long as it is serving the mission. Discard it when it is not. Deadlines help alleviate boredom and procrastination, but they can introduce anxiety and undermine the project when used aggressively.

As I write this, I have given myself a deadline to finish this chapter. This helps me to offset my tendency to procrastinate. I am making good progress under this self-imposed pressure. My timelines help keep me moving forward.

If you find yourself trying to work on one project but distracted by a dozen other tasks that also need doing, it can help create a schedule. In a calendar planner, mark out what period you will work on one thing and another block of time for the next thing on your list. Then follow the schedule. If you do this, it will help. When your subconscious mind begins to trust that you will follow the plan and the important things are on the schedule, it will relax. When there is no rhyme or reason to your attention, your subconscious mind may try to assist by repeatedly reminding you of important and urgent tasks but at the worst possible times, like just as you are falling asleep at night.

Even with a schedule, this may still happen occasionally. If you know that the item you thought of is already on the agenda that you are following, it is easier to dismiss the thought and focus back on what you are supposed to work on right now. If an important idea occurs to you that is not already on your planner, pause to update your calendar. Now your subconscious knows that this new idea will be addressed, and it will allow you to return your focus to the scheduled work. Please note that this only works if you follow your to-do list for long enough that your subconscious mind begins to trust the process.

Overcoming Inertia

The longer we sit still, the harder it becomes to initiate forward movement. Such situations are the perfect place to practice using commitments. Choose a small, easily-attained goal and a short timeline, and then commit to it as if your life depended upon it. It does! Once committed, follow through to success. Make your commitment sacred, and do not fail. If you succeed, you have already won the hardest battle of the campaign. Celebrate! Then do it again. Commit to another small step and do whatever it takes to succeed, and slowly you will build momentum.

When I hear a new yoga student tell me that they plan to practice yoga for an hour a day for the rest of their life, I cringe. This commitment is flawed for several reasons. First of all, an hour is a lot of time when you are in a crisis. There may come a day when it is easy to convince yourself that you do not have an hour to spare. Then you break your commitment and seriously damage whatever belief you had in yourself.

Secondly, the benefit to self-esteem comes upon completion of a goal. If your goal is to do yoga every day for the rest of your life, you must wait until you die to know if you kept your commitment.

I try to steer such students toward a more intelligent commitment. The hardest step on a journey is the first. It can be challenging to break free of inertia. On a bad day, you are looking for an excuse not to start. The most common reason for not starting is a lack of time. Instead of committing to one hour, commit to at least five minutes of yoga every day.

Even on the worst of days, come hell or high water, take five minutes to practice yoga. You will find that it is easy to stretch five minutes into twenty or more once you start. But regardless, you show up for your five minutes. Do not have an infinite or indeterminate timeline. Shorter timelines increase the odds of success, especially for those who are not already firm in their commitments.

So here is the finished commitment: "I will practice at least five minutes of yoga every day for one week." Remember that to find Flow, your goal needs to be challenging but not impossible. If it is too much to commit to, make it easier. Start with at least five minutes of practice on five of the next seven days. Give yourself a little wiggle room if you need it.

Once you have your goal, commit to it, not just in words but also with your heart and soul. Make this a sacred pact, and then no matter what happens, do not let yourself down. Once you commit, it is no longer about the goal; it is about the commitment itself. Track your progress, and when complete, celebrate your success. Then choose a new goal and commit to it.

As you begin to believe in the power of your commitment, it becomes a force unto itself. Do not slip. Do not get careless. Choose your battles carefully, and then make sure you win every one of them. There are some people whose very word has the power to create the future. These people seldom commit and never carelessly, but when they do, even the gods step aside.

"The difference between involvement and commitment is like ham and eggs. The chicken is involved; the pig is committed." ~ Martina Navratilova

Celebrating Success

After completing each goal, take the time to celebrate! Match the celebration to the goal. In achieving a process goal, like holding downward-facing dog for a certain number of breaths in your yoga practice, a simple reward such as relaxing in a child's pose might be sufficient.

With a tactical goal, the celebration should be a little larger. If you are regularly late for work, aim to be at work five minutes early every day for a week. Choose a motivating reward, like getting to watch five minutes of cat videos on your smartphone each day that you arrive to work early. If you complete the week without missing a single day, treat yourself to buying your beloved some fresh catnip.

At the strategic goal level, success comes less often and is celebrated with more care. Upon completing your junior year in college and meeting the GPA goal you set for yourself, you might enroll in scuba lessons in the campus pool.

Upon completing a mission goal, like graduating with a degree in marine biology, the celebration is even more extravagant, perhaps a seven-day vacation snorkeling in the Azores.

There are three critical attributes to celebrating success:

1. The celebration must be commensurate with the level of challenge.

2. The celebration must be chosen simultaneously with the goal or soon after that. This way, the anticipated celebration can serve as motivation when you are struggling to find Flow.

3. Just as a goal is in service to the goals above it, so to your celebration. The celebration must move you closer to, not further from, your next goal.

The third of these tenets is the most important to understand and implement. If you do not consciously choose the nature of your celebration, you will select it unconsciously. This permits the rise of a shadow goal that undermines your higher aspirations. Imagine that you go on a diet and successfully lose 20 pounds in 20 days. At the moment of victory, you could easily decide to celebrate with a bowl of ice cream. Imagine you just met your goal of saving a thousand dollars. If you are not careful, you will celebrate by spending money on something you had previously denied yourself. I am sure you recognize this problem, if not in yourself, certainly in others.

So, before you succeed, make sure you have chosen a specific celebration that moves you even closer to your mission goal. For instance, if you lose 20 pounds, celebrate with a new swimsuit! If you save the thousand dollars, reward yourself by joining a friend on their sailboat for the weekend.

"The original meaning of the word resolution means to 'break into parts.' Think about that as you make your New Year's resolutions. Break the big ones down. Break the little ones down. Every step is a victory. Don't you dare wait until the finish line to celebrate. Life happens along the journey, not just at the finish line." ~ Toni Sorenson

Chapter Six

FLOW IS THE ANSWER

The Case Against Fear

There is a common perception that fear is necessary, that fear helps us survive, and that we would not survive in the absence of fear. So, let's take a closer look at fear.

I do not feel any fear when walking on the sidewalk while cars speed by, even on a narrow sidewalk with fast-moving vehicles. Despite my lack of fear, I do not step out in front of a speeding car. Why? Because that would be stupid! My survival is not the result of a fear of automobiles. It is simple logic - I love life, and I am not ready to die. This is sufficient motivation for me to look both ways before crossing. It is not a fear of failure that keeps me safe on the street; it is the pursuit of excellence. Show me someone terrified of cars, and I will show you someone more likely to get hit by one crossing the road.

Acrophobia is the fear of heights. Some argue that we have a genetic fear of falling so that we will avoid dangerous places. Thus, our fear is necessary for the survival of our species. If I am close to a cliff's edge, I am fine. But if I think about falling, then I get dizzy and weak, increasing my risk of falling. Mountain goats have little if any, fear of heights especially compared to domestic animals. This is no coincidence. The mountain goats that were scared of heights did not live long enough to pass on their DNA.

New research shows that many types of anxiety have a genetic component. The Iroquois Indians, specifically Mohawks from the Kahnawake reservation near Montreal, were and are still famous for their fearlessness in the face of great heights. Part of their ability is undoubtedly due to culture, pushing into fear to build a tolerance for fear (expanding their Flow window), but part may also be genetic.

When it came time to build the skyscrapers in New York, Mohawks led the way, walking casually along steel beams suspended thousands of feet above the streets below. It was those with the least fear who were least likely to fall. Perhaps looking forward to seeing their kids after they finished work was sufficient motivation to keep them from jumping.

To those who say that fear is necessary, I would offer a different take. Perhaps the function of fear is not to protect the prey, but for the sake of the predator! In the absence of fear, almost any prey animal can get in one well-aimed kick or jab and take out the predator's eye or bruise its thigh. If a prey animal injures the predator, even slightly, the predator could starve before healing sufficiently to resume hunting.

There are far fewer predators than prey, and the predator maintains the balance of the herd, weeding out the slowest, weakest animals and thus strengthening the gene pool. Maybe fear is nature's way of helping make sure the predator does not get hurt! Fear among prey animals may play a key role in maintaining the balance between gazelles and lions, benefiting both species, as well as the ecosystem that evolves around them! Fear certainly does little to help the individual rabbit, immobilized as the cat approaches, while holding its gaze.

Ancient warriors and competitive athletes have always known that fear destroys performance.

The Cure for Stress

To the degree that you can gain control over your own goals, you can live a stress-free life. Imagine a world where everyone learned how to understand and control their own goals, to live in Flow.

While it may be difficult to gain complete control of your goals, it is relatively easy to make small improvements in this skill, resulting in improved life quality.

In one recent survey, 66% of employees admitted to trouble focusing on work tasks due to stress. This results in reduced productivity, and worse, mistakes that can bring down entire institutions!

Dr. Nicholas Cummings, Chief Psychologist at Kaiser Permanente, cites a 1981 landmark study reviewing the charts of Kaiser-Permanente patients, which concluded that "60-90% of physician visits reflect emotional distress and somatization." Stress has been called the "health epidemic of the 21st century" by the World Health Organization and is estimated to cost American businesses up to $300 billion a year.

These studies do not even begin to address patients' and their families' pain and suffering resulting from avoidable illness. If we could move the needle even slightly, increasing the collective Flow of entire populations and reducing stress, the results might be staggering. Just as fear begets fear, Flow begets Flow.

The Crisis in Healthcare

Perhaps the most fundamental and overlooked problem with our healthcare system is that it is primarily rooted in the Circle of Failure! The goal is to help people avoid getting sick and dying. If someone is not currently ill, there is no real direction provided. The patient is

left to drift along until they have a medical emergency. Then the healthcare system kicks into action with a vengeance. The patient's life turns upside down, with changes to their diet, therapy, drugs, and surgery. If they recover, urgency recedes, and they go back to sleep - until the next crisis!

A healthcare model based on the Blue Dot of Success looks very different. Here, we aspire to be truly healthy in body, mind, and spirit. We do not wait for a crisis. We make continuous adjustments, always looking for how we can improve our health. Whether we are sick or healthy, we are still looking for ways to improve.

As practiced widely in the People's Republic of China, Taiwan, South and North Koreas, Japan, Vietnam, and Hong Kong, traditional medicine has a reward system that is perfectly aligned with the Blue Dot of Success philosophy. Patients pay their physicians to keep them healthy. If the patient falls ill, they stop paying their doctor! This is an excellent example of applying the Blue Dot of Success model to medicine. By contrast, the Western healthcare industry profits more when we are sick.

Rather than waging war on bacteria, consider seeking balance. We cannot live without bacteria. If the bacterial communities on our skin are in harmony, our skin is healthier. When the bacteria in our G.I. system live in balance, we are healthier physically, emotionally, and mentally.

Rather than just trying to prevent specific diseases like measles, pay a little more attention to restoring balance to the immune system. When we suppress the immune system, we are more susceptible to a variety of diseases. When the immune system is overly aggressive, we suffer from a rash of autoimmune diseases: lupus, fibromyalgia, arthritis, inflammatory bowel disease, to name just a few. The immune system is sensitive to environmental changes, including emotions like love, boredom, or anxiety. Perhaps a little more Flow in our lives might help balance our immune system and improve well-being.

Yoga and other Eastern philosophies can complement the Western scientific model. The West focuses on taking sick people and bringing them up to average health but then abandons them until the next crisis. Most research looks at how to cure disease. On the other hand, Eastern philosophies traditionally asked how people who are already healthy in body and spirit can become even better: stronger, more flexible, healthier, more energetic, mentally and emotionally resilient, focused, happier, and eventually, for those who truly excel, the possibility of samadhi, or enlightenment.

America is often called "the melting pot" with good cause. In the past decade, many Western doctors and scientists have begun to integrate Eastern ideas and philosophies into their practice. Rather than just studying disease, scientists are also studying peak performers and asking how we can help more people to thrive. At the same time, those practicing Eastern traditions, like yoga, benefit from Western science.

Yoga was historically considered a path to oneness. Over the last century, yoga has earned growing recognition as a therapeutic tool. More recently, Western medicine has reached the same conclusion. As a result, yoga therapy is gaining in popularity across the U.S. and the world. Besides yoga therapy, other healing traditions such as Ayurveda and acupuncture focus on promoting health and balance rather than avoiding illness. Many Americans who pay for medical insurance still choose to pay out of pocket for such alternative forms of medicine that have at their heart the Blue Dot of Success.

Competition

A competitor whose goal is not to lose is more likely to lose. In part, this is because they will tend to practice just enough to avoid defeat, which is, after all, their goal. So sooner or later, they will underestimate an opponent or overestimate their own preparations and lose. There is also the inherent problem with negative goals of boredom and fear. If the opponent is better than them, they will suffer in training and in competition from anxiety. If the opponent is weaker than them, they will suffer from boredom and carelessness.

In comparison, following the Blue Dot of Success model, a competitor with a positive goal is not affected by their opponent's relative quality. Their motivation to train and compete is intrinsic. Moreover, it is more likely that they will be in Flow while training and during competition.

Education

There is a substantial variety of quality of our educational systems in the USA, both between schools and individual teachers. Many of these schools and teachers are fully committed to helping students find Flow. However, some teachers and schools are firmly rooted in the Circle of Failure. I have visited many classrooms where students' dominant energy is a mixture of boredom and anxiety with little, if any, Flow.

"Teaching to the test" was one of the worst unanticipated side effects of the push to standardize testing in schools. Tests serve one legitimate purpose. They provide feedback on students' skill levels, allowing the teacher to choose new goals to help restore Flow. In this respect, tests are helpful. When we teach students to perform well on a test, we have inverted the process. Now the test drives education rather than measuring its effectiveness.

When we judge a student by their performance on a test, it can damage both the exceptional student and the struggling student alike. The extraordinary student finds they do not have to work as hard to make good grades. On the other hand, students who are working hard, but still struggling to test well, get discouraged.

Test-taking ability is not a good measure of a student's prospects. A good work ethic and E.Q. (emotional intelligence) are far better indicators of future success than I.Q. A genius without a strong work ethic is doomed to failure. Someone with a good work ethic can become a productive and even essential member of society once they find their niche. Over a longer timeline, it is the tortoise that wins the race, not the hare.

Instead of praising a student for being smart or punishing them for being slow (attributes that they have little control over), praise them when they engage in the process, work hard, or find their Flow.

If teachers, supported by administrators and lawmakers, were to shift their focus to the Blue Dot of Success, where each student has a clear and challenging goal to pursue, they might be surprised at the students' buy-in. If they adopt a Flow model, they might succeed in eliminating boredom and anxiety in the classroom. Children in Flow soak up knowledge like a sponge.

If you are a teacher, it all starts with you. Learn how to put yourself in Flow. If you are bored or scared, your students will know it and behave accordingly. Once you master your own goals and find Flow, help your students find Flow. But do not stop there. It is just a matter of time before your students end up in a classroom with a teacher who is not in Flow and does not instill Flow in their students. Before your students graduate from your classroom, teach them how to put themselves in Flow. Look for Flow in your classroom and compliment it.

Personal Learning

"In a time of drastic change, it is the learners who inherit the future. The learned usually find themselves equipped to live in a world that no longer exists." ~ Eric Hoffer

Feedback is essential to learning. In yoga, if you are paying attention, you will hear your body talking to you. As you stretch your hamstrings, you might feel pleasure, discomfort, or even pain. If we pay attention to feedback, we can learn from experience.

If you find a senior citizen who has never used a computer and sit them in front of a screen with a keyboard, they usually freeze. They are scared to touch the keyboard because they might make a mistake. This results in no feedback and, therefore, no learning.

Contrast that to a five-year-old child who, likewise, has never used a computer. The child immediately starts hitting keys, and the computer provides them feedback. The five-year-old might make a hundred mistakes on the first day, but check back in a couple of months, and you might be surprised by what they can do with your computer.

The secret to learning is a willingness to make mistakes and then learn from them. You must choose to value learning over performance.

Six steps to learning:

Step 1: Deliberately put yourself into a situation where you do not know what to do. (If you already know what to do, you are not in a learning environment.)

Step 2: Do something - anything! Isolate one variable and play with it. Do not change more than one variable at a time if you can avoid it.

Step 3: Listen to and make sure you understand the feedback, both positive and negative. Do not think of negative feedback as a failure and positive feedback as a success, but rather see both positive and negative feedback as the information you can use to adjust course.

Step 4: If feedback is positive, continue in that direction. If negative, try something different.

Step 5: Return to Step 2 and choose a new variable to explore. Repeat the process of cycling through these steps until you succeed.

Step 6: When you have mastered the new material, celebrate! But also recognize that you are no longer in a learning environment. When you are ready to resume learning, go back to Step 1 by deliberately putting yourself into a situation that you do not understand but wish to.

Let's look at this process using our models. Notice that most people hang out in their comfort zone as boredom increases. Then they launch themselves deep into the unknown, triggering anxiety. Then they retreat to comfort and boredom. Learning shuts down when we are bored or scared. We see this pattern in adults all the time.

Compare this previous model to the following one. If you look at the Circle of Failure, the Poor Learning chart, and the Flow window together, you can see how they relate.

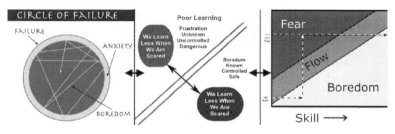

Likewise, if you look at the Blue Dot of Success, the Excellent Learning Environment, and the Deep Flow model that follows, you will see the similarities. In all three models, we do not wait to be bored or scared. Instead, we constantly adjust goals to stay in Flow and focus on success.

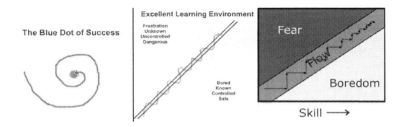

Science

Science used to be rooted in the Blue Dot of Success model. Two hundred years ago, the scientist's Blue Dot was the search for truth. Even then, there were ego-driven feuds between famous scientific figures, but they still aspired to pursue truth in general. Over time, science moved from a hobby driven by curiosity, and a passion for discovery, into a career.

Today, many scientists are driven by curiosity to pursue the truth. But others become distracted by the potential for failure. If a position they have championed is proven wrong, there is money at stake. Funding dries up. Tenure is withheld, employees laid off, and their children may have to settle for more affordable education.

Many scientists find themselves trapped in a Circle of Failure. Confronted with data that conflict with their position, they might ignore it. They might be tempted to promote a project they know to be a long shot over more promising work due to funding considerations.

For those who can stay firmly and passionately focused on revealing the truth, following their Blue Dot of Success from one discovery to the next, a life of Flow is its own reward. Of course, science is not a hobby for most scientists in this era, and they must pay the rent. Each time a scientist values the avoidance of mistakes over seeking truth, we all lose out. At its heart, science should be driven by curiosity and Flow.

Politics and the Art of Avoidance

Many politicians consider politics a career. Success for them is vague, but failure – not getting reelected – is clearly defined. They are entrenched in the Circle of Failure. They ignore issues until there is a crisis and then "boldly" prescribe radical solutions. They insist on declaring war on abstract ideas that can never be won, like poverty and terror. That is the whole point! Success is so vague that they can never be judged or held accountable. Such politicians are easily corrupted. Because they do not have firmly held beliefs to anchor them, they can turn on a dime and support the highest bidder.

When politicians follow their own Blue Dot of Success, they focus on accomplishing what needs to be done for the greater good of those they lead, both now and into the future. Seeing a problem on the distant horizon, they take action to avert it. If they do their job well, there is no crisis, and no one notices or credits them. Such a politician knows that they may not get reelected, especially when taking difficult but necessary positions. They focus on what they need to accomplish rather than on trying to avoid failure.

Why are there so many of the former and so few of the latter? We, the voters, are to blame. We get the government we deserve. If we vote for politicians who campaign to avoid mistakes, we should not be surprised when they govern in the same manner.

Diets

Some diets are essential, especially when prescribed by healthcare professionals for ill patients, like diabetics. But for the rest of us, diets can cause more harm - physically, mentally, and emotionally - not only to ourselves but to our loved ones who are also affected by our behavior.

Most diets fail because they are based on the Circle of Avoidance. We avoid certain foods, and we limit the amounts of others. The focus of the mind is kept on that which we deny ourselves. This may work in the short term, but over time, we are feeding the "White Horse" at the expense of the "Red Rose." We become obsessed with what we are giving up. Once we reach a target weight and the crisis has been averted, we go back to our old habits, drifting aimlessly along until the next crisis and the next diet.

When we apply the Blue Dot of Success to our diet, we focus on a clear and positive health goal. Rather than denying types and quantities of food, we focus on identifying and eating the right foods. It is a lifestyle of mindfulness, not another diet. It is important to note that we do not focus on denying ourselves certain forbidden foods, which puts us back in the Circle of Failure. Instead, we keep our focus on eating good foods. Are old patterns are now seen as distractions and will tend to fall away without effort.

On the rare occasion that we eat something that takes us in the "wrong" direction, it is not a crisis. We do not waste time or energy on guilt. Instead, we just adjust course and continue to spiral back in toward our Blue Dot of Success.

War on Drugs

Once again, we see the Circle of Failure in our approach to drug rehabilitation. Don't relapse! Many programs focus on all the bad things that will happen if their patients go back to their old habits. Instead, help them realize the limitless options possible if they focus on and pursue success.

A landmark study on addiction has influenced many of our drug policies. Researchers offered caged rats a choice of food or drugs. The rats chose drugs over food, slowly starving to death. It was only recently that a scientist revisited that study from a Blue Dot of Success model. He transformed the cage into a rat's version of Disneyland. Tunnels, wheels, tubes, other rats to play with, and gave the rats the same choice between food and drugs. These rats chose food. This may help explain why drug use in prison is such a problem.

Perhaps if we created better environments for people to live in, environments where there is hope for a better life, we might have fewer new addicts. I do not think a nicer rat cage will cure the addict who has already structurally altered their brain, but it wouldn't hurt! And in conjunction with other therapies, it might just make the difference between successful treatment and relapse.

One final thought on drugs and Flow: Most people turn to drugs out of boredom or fear. If we teach people how to find Flow, they might be less inclined to seek drugs to escape boredom or fear. The Circle of Failure is so ubiquitous that you can find it almost anywhere you look. Root out those areas in your own life where you are motivated by the avoidance of failure, and redirect that energy to some better, worthier cause.

War on Crime

Recidivism rates are typically used to measure the efficacy of criminal rehabilitation. When we use failure rates to assess progress, we will reward those who do just enough to avoid failure while ignoring any further progress. Success is vague, but failure is clearly defined. This is another example of a Circle of Failure. It leads to complacency, followed by crisis and radical action. This is true for the criminal, who can be ignored between the crises. It is equally true for the system as a whole.

A Blue Dot of Success model focuses not on preventing criminals from relapsing but rather on helping them become successful, productive members of society. Here the focus is on what success looks like, rather than on failure.

A Beacon of Light

In every one of these areas – healthcare, education, science, diet, politics, drugs, crime – you will find people who are achieving miraculous results. What do they have in common? Deep Flow! How are they finding Deep Flow in themselves and inspiring those around them? They have a clear and inspirational vision of what could be, and they are willing to make mistakes and learn as they pursue that vision.

Let me share one example with you that illustrates many of the principles we have discussed. Mildred Lisette Norman was born in 1908. Thirty years later, she had a profound experience while walking in the woods. Mildred walked through the night and into the dawn, turning a corner in her life. Over the next 14 years, she gradually simplified her life. In 1952, she made history by becoming the first woman to walk the Appalachian Trail's entire length in one season. In the process, she gained clarity on her vision and mission. The next year, she donned a sweatshirt that would soon become famous. On the back, it said "Walking Coast to Coast for Peace," and on the front, it said "Peace Pilgrim" in large bold font. Then she stepped onto the pavement and started the first of seven cross-country pilgrimages. She stopped counting at 20,000 miles, but it has been estimated that she walked over 43,000 miles for peace.

The Peace Pilgrim, as she became known, was one of my mother's heroes. Rather than watching the news and worrying about the world's fate, the Peace Pilgrim chose to act for world peace in her own small way. Her vision was to share a simple message with those she encountered on the road: "This is the way of peace: Overcome evil with good, falsehood with truth, and hatred with love."

But it is her "rules for the road" that I find most remarkable. She did not carry any possessions other than a water bottle, no clothes beyond walking shoes, pants, and her famous sweatshirt (no coat or umbrella). She did not carry money, not even a dime for an emergency phone call. She never asked for food, but if it was offered, she never turned it down. If she had eaten recently, she would still make time to share food and company when invited. The longest she went without anyone offering her food was 17 days, so she fasted for 17 days. At the request of a chiropractor, who wanted to see how healthy people responded to fasting, she went 45 days without food under his supervision. It was during this period that she said she learned how to "pray without ceasing."

She walked, regardless of weather, and never asked for shelter but accepted it when offered. The closest she came to dying on one of her pilgrimages was in a blizzard. She spent the night curled up into a ball in the shelter of an overpass. She later shared that she had felt God's presence, warming her through the night.

The Peace Pilgrim never asked for a ride, but she never turned one down if offered. She never asked herself if it was safe to accept a ride. If God opened a door, she stepped through. Often, a car going the wrong direction would see her walking along a small country road, miles from anywhere, and would stop to offer her a ride. She would always accept, and then they would talk for hours, traveling in the wrong direction. When dropped off, she would turn around and resume her journey, perhaps taking several days to get back to where she had accepted the ride.

Mission in Service to Vision

What can we learn about goals from the Peace Pilgrim's example? If we have a strong vision, do we need a mission and strategy? Yes! Imagine if the Peace Pilgrim did not have a mission, and instead, she just wandered around talking to people randomly about her vision for world peace. She would merely be another homeless person, and few people would have stopped to listen. Her mission of walking across America created structure and opportunities for sharing her vision of world peace with more people. The combination of vision and mission was so powerful that this former housewife, without a penny to her name, came to the personal attention of J. Edgar Hoover and the FBI. She was eventually nominated for the Nobel Peace Prize.

Her mission of walking across the continent played a crucial role in success. But what did the Peace Pilgrim do when offered a ride in the wrong direction? Without hesitation, she got in the car. Why? Because she never lost sight of her vision: connecting with people and sharing her vision for world peace. What direction they were driving in was inconsequential to this vision. This is why it is so important to be clear in prioritizing your goals.

Process Goals for the Road

In the end, it was not just the quality of her vision or the success of her mission that changed people's lives and elevated a hitchhiker to international fame. It was her capacity for Deep Flow! What she referred to as her "rules for the road" correspond to process goals. Do not turn down food. Do not ask for food. Never turn down a ride. Never ask for a ride. Do not carry money. All of these rules for the road helped her to stay in Flow. In the moment, step by step, one conversation at a time, she shared her true self with strangers. In her, they saw themselves as she saw them: children of God and part of the field of unconditional love. This was the universe that she chose to live within.

What can we learn from the Peace Pilgrim's example? Use process goals to stay in Flow while holding tightly to your vision, and lightly to the goals in between.

Maslow's Hierarchy of Needs

"The greater danger for most of us is not that our aim is too high and we miss it, but that it is too low and we hit it." ~ Michelangelo Buonarroti

Abraham Maslow first introduced the iconic diagram below in 1943.

Maslow's Hierarchy of Needs

It is usually just referred to as "Maslow's Hierarchy of Needs." Maslow argued that it is a mistake to focus on higher needs before satisfying those needs below it. On the other hand, once we have fulfilled those lower needs, we must endeavor to set our sights higher, working our way up through the hierarchy with self-actualization as the ultimate goal.

The first level of the pyramid is comprised of physiological needs. These can also be organized into their own hierarchy. The importance of shelter is hard to pin down. It usually is the least important but might move up as high as number two in a blizzard. The rest are ranked from least to most important: food, sleep, water, oxygen. You can live without food for several weeks. Eleven days is the record for a person to survive sleep deprivation. Four days is about as long as you can live without water. But, the undisputed champion of needs is oxygen. When prevented from breathing, most people will feel panic set in almost immediately and irreparable damage to the brain in less than ten minutes.

Where to Start?

To get the greatest return on your investment, reinforce the weakest and the most important links in your chain. Following Maslow's Hierarchy of Needs, the answer is obvious. Start with breath control, and then work your way up through the pyramid.

When we consider how critical breathing is to our health, why do most people pay so little attention to it? As you might have guessed, the answer is that they are operating from a Circle of Avoidance. When it comes to the breath, failure is clearly defined; a panic attack or even death. Success is vague and expressed in terms of not failing. So they go through life not noticing breath until breathing becomes difficult, and then they panic. For these individuals, breath awareness is either boring or scary. They are not in Flow with breath!

I have helped thousands of students to improve their breathing. The first step is to replace the Circle of Avoidance with the Blue Dot of Success. Make your goal to maximize your breathing potential. No matter how well you are already breathing, there is room for improvement. First, learn how to breathe with different areas of your lungs, especially the diaphragm. Then learn to put these areas together in different sequences for differing effects. Next, work to control the rhythm of your breath (the length of your inhalation, retention, exhalation, and retention). Increase the variety of breathing patterns that you can sustain comfortably and without effort. Learn how to slow down your overall rhythm or speed it up. One of my favorite teachers, Rama Vernon, could speed up her breathing to 60 breaths a minute (breath of fire) and then turn around and slow down to one breath every four minutes. She was comfortable at either extreme and everywhere in between.

As you begin to increase your breath control, you will see immediate improvements in your stamina, physical health, mental health, emotional health, concentration, creativity, and ability to meditate. The most important advice I can give you when it comes to pranayama is to prioritize finding Flow while practicing breath control. If you are bored, choose a more advanced practice. If you feel anxious, choose a more comfortable practice. When you learn to enjoy pranayama, you will know that you are on the right track.

When working with breath control, it is recommended that you work with a qualified teacher, especially at the beginning of your exploration and later when you begin to explore breath retention. Some yoga teachers may be experienced in teaching pranayama, but most are not. If you cannot find a qualified yoga teacher to help, a voice coach can teach you the basics of diaphragmatic breathing, which is the best place to start.

Next, turn your attention to water quality and quantity. Learn to yawn regularly, which helps move fluid into and through connective tissues to hydrate the fascia. Cultivate regular exercise (of course, I favor yoga, but any physical activity you enjoy is acceptable). Then turn some attention to your diet. Following the Blue Dot of Success model, rather than denying yourself bad foods, seek out and explore the fantastic variety of healthy foods available to us. Create a physical space in which you feel comfortable physically, mentally, and emotionally, not just a shelter but a home.

Assuming that you are meeting all of these needs, does that mean you are satisfied? Of course not; now you want security. So, now you are satisfied? No, you still desire friendship. Is that enough to be happy? No, next you long for increased self-esteem, compassion, and love. Okay, are we there yet? Not yet, because if all of these needs are met, the desire for self-knowledge and self-control will take center stage. This will lead to a desire for wisdom, and the wise long for God (illumination, samadhi, enlightenment, or self-actualization). Start where you are, and continue working your way up through the pyramid.

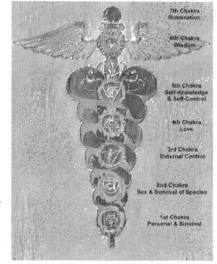

"Don't ask what the world needs. Ask what makes you come alive and go do it. Because what the world needs is people who have come alive." ~ Howard Thurman

Maslow 2.0

Maslow's pyramid is often compared to the much older human psychology models of the caduceus and the seven chakras, which date back at least as far as the Indus Valley Civilization in ancient antiquity. The primary difference is that the chakra model's top three levels are self-knowledge, wisdom, and illumination (or variations on this theme). Maslow's pyramid only has one top level grouping he called "Self-Actualization."

Few people know that Maslow revised his pyramid later in life. He delineated the top level of his earlier pyramid into three parts: cognitive needs, aesthetic needs, and at the very top, self-actualization. He then added one more level above that which he called transcendence. These later models are even closer to the classic chakra model.

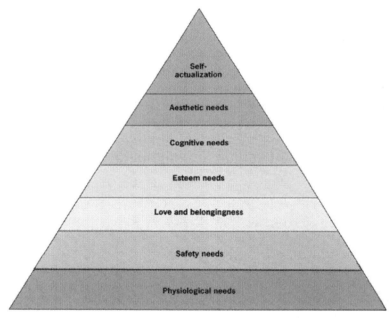

Note that cognitive needs correspond to the fifth chakra of self-knowledge; aesthetic needs (appreciation and search for beauty, balance, and form) correspond to the sixth chakra of wisdom; and of course, self-actualization corresponds to the seventh chakra of illumination.

It is interesting to note that Maslow grouped the first four layers of his pyramid into what he termed "deficiency needs." Here, motivation decreases as the need is satisfied. After you finish a large meal, the motivation to search for more food diminishes. However, he labeled the three highest levels, cognitive, aesthetic, and self-actualization, as "growth needs." Here motivation increases as these needs are met. A growing appreciation for beauty, balance, and understanding increases motivation for further growth rather than satisfying it. This accelerating motivation provides the momentum necessary to transcend self.

"The intelligent want self-control; children want candy." ~ Rumi

I find it fascinating that the chakra model pre-dates Maslow by at least a thousand years. Most scholars think it is much older, perhaps two to three thousand years old. However, based upon recent findings at a dig in Turkey, I suspect that these ideas may be far older.

A stone carving found at the Gobekli Tepe excavation in Eastern Turkey is estimated to be over 10,000 years old. It is called the "Birdman of Gobekli Tepe". The image is easy to find with a web search. The carving combines the caduceus's essential elements (two snakes crossing six times) and the chakras (six circles distributed from the pelvic floor to the third eye) into one image. A pair of wings emerges from either side of the figures head, which is where he gets his name "Birdman" from.

If you need a little structure to help you choose and organize your goals, either Maslow or the seven-chakra model is an excellent place to start. Remember, do not get too far ahead of yourself. If you live on the streets and are not content to do so, focus on your most immediate needs of food and shelter. Once you have addressed those needs, raise your gaze higher.

"It must be borne in mind that the tragedy of life doesn't lie in not reaching your goal. It lies in having no goal to reach. It is not a calamity to die with dreams unfulfilled, but it is a calamity not to dream. It is not a disgrace to reach the stars, but it is a disgrace not to have any stars to reach. Not failure, but low aim, is the real sin." ~Benjamin Mays

Three Wishes

A friend who is a lawyer took a phone call from a prospective client. The new client was an ex-intelligence officer and needed help negotiating a deal with his former employer.

Of course, being who he was, his idea of an interview was not so straightforward. "If you were granted three wishes, what would you wish for?" he asked the lawyer. "Wisdom" was the reply. "Ahhh... yes... very good, and what would you wish for with the last two wishes?" the client asked. "I think I will wait for the first wish to be granted before I use my last two wishes," replied my friend.

A wise person acts on their heart's desire. A smart person searches for this knowledge before acting. A fool is too busy acting to look.

Hopefully, as we grow older, we grow a little less foolish and gain some degree of knowledge and wisdom. As we do, it is important to revisit our goals occasionally. Step back, and dispassionately from a distance, take a look at your desires and plans to make sure they are still a good fit with your life.

The dreams of a seven-year-old are often not the dreams of a teenager, a parent, or a grandparent. At each stage of life, our goals should reflect who we wish to become and not who we used to be.

Helical Orbits

Imagine an astronaut orbiting around the moon. According to Johannes Kepler's laws of planetary motion, the astronaut's orbit is elliptical. For anyone standing on the moon, this would be true. But from

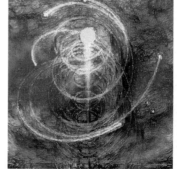

the Earth, we see that the moon is circling the Earth. Therefore, the astronaut is orbiting the moon's path around the earth, creating a spiral rather than an ellipse. In turn, the moon is spiraling around the path of the Earth. The Earth spirals around the sun's path, which spirals around the galaxy's path. This is called the Helical Model of the solar system.

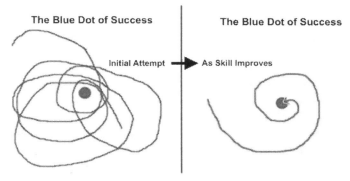

When you apply the Blue Dot of Success model to your mission board, you find the same infinite and beautiful complexity. Small goals spiral around the paths created by larger goals, which spiral around still larger goals. And at the center, holding it all together is the vision. When we take the time to organize our goals throughout all levels, a similar fractal-like structure emerges.

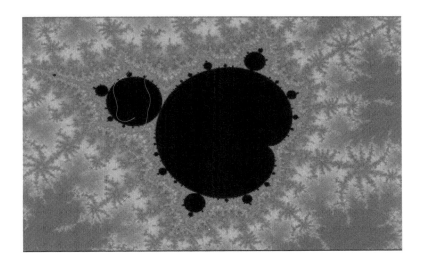

159

This image models the complex boundary between order and chaos. This is an apt metaphor for the flow model, which exists at a similar boundary, between boredom and fear.

On Death and Dying

I recommend using the Flow and Blue Dot of Success models in small, everyday situations to practice and improve your skill at controlling goals to maintain Flow and manifest success. As you become more adept at managing your goals, you will find that you can use these skills to stay in Flow in more challenging situations. Now let's see how these models hold up when applied to such extreme conditions. Setting goals is easy. Letting go of toxic goals is the real challenge, and never more so than dealing with mortality.

Imagine Joe is crossing a parking lot late at night. Someone steps in front of him and puts a gun to his head, intending to pull the trigger. Joe might have been in Flow a few minutes earlier, but this circumstance will most likely be met by anxiety. If you are bored or scared, it is always a result of a toxic goal.

First, take an inventory of skills. If Joe is an Aikido black belt or a psychotherapist, his skills might be adequate to this situation, and he might still be in Flow. Let's assume, however, that his talents for this situation are marginal.

Now take a look at Joe's goal. In all probability, Joe did not analyze the situation and choose an appropriate response. More likely, an unconscious goal rose unbidden, bringing with it anxiety. Joe does not want to die! This is why he is scared! He has allowed a toxic goal to hijack his attention. How do we know this goal is toxic? "Know the tree by its fruits!" If you are bored or scared, you are under the influence of a toxic goal.

Why is the goal of not dying toxic? For starters, from the Flow model, we can see that Joe has set his goal too high for his lack of skills. From the Blue Dot model, we can see that this is a negative goal. He is focused on what he does not want to happen. Thus, he is operating within the Circle of Failure. Failure is clearly defined as death. Success is vague, anything that does not involve dying. We can also see that this goal is external to his locus of control. Joe has little influence over whether or not the assailant pulls the trigger. The goal is also about holding onto the status quo, present moment situation, rather than looking forward to the future. Not wanting to die is a toxic goal for Joe at this moment.

Remember the principle that the Circle of Failure manifests failure? Joe's goal of not dying is responsible for his fear. Fear clouds judgment robs us of strength, immobilizes prey, and empowers predators. Joe's goal of not dying is about to get him killed! Holding onto a toxic goal is not logical. However, as we have discussed previously, toxic goals can be sticky. It is not easy to let go of the goal of not dying, but it is possible. If Joe succeeds in releasing his goal of not dying, he will be free to choose a new goal. To find Flow, choose goals that are challenging but within our ability.

If you know that you will die at some point, what becomes important to you about your death? Do you want your final moments to be ones of fear, anger, bitterness, despair, or FLOW? If Joe were to think about how he wanted to die, he would probably agree that dying while in a Flow state would be preferable to dying while full of fear.

So back to the parking lot. This is Joe's chance! It may have come a little earlier than he planned, but whether it is here and now in a parking lot, or forty years from now in a nursing home, facing death will never be easy!

Instead of his last moments being fear-based, Joe could choose to focus on his own Blue Dot, on finding Flow. He may not be able to control his assailant's trigger finger, but he can choose to control his reaction to this situation. It is not easy, but it is possible. Rather than Joe spending his final moments wishing he could live longer; he could choose to admit that his fate is not in his hands. Accepting that there is a good chance he is about to die; he could decide to make the best use of his remaining time. So, he chooses to remember those he loved and who loved him, to feel grateful for the gift of life, and look forward to the next adventure, whatever that might be. Perhaps Joe is successful and finds Flow.

Now Joe looks at his assailant, pointing a gun at his head. This is probably the last face Joe will ever see. Perhaps he wonders what this young person's path has been and realizes that his assailant's life has probably been considerably harsher than his own. Knowing this, Joe might even feel compassion. Imagine if Joe made eye contact with his assailant, and from his heart, with love, told the young man, "Whatever you have to do right now, I want you to know that it is okay, and I forgive you." It is not the words that matter but the source. If Joe is in Deep Flow, feeling unconditional love for the man holding the gun, what happens to the young man's ability to pull the trigger?

Fear empowers the predatory nature of others. Fearlessness and love have the opposite effect. This may be the first time this young man has ever been on the receiving end of unconditional love. Perhaps he drops the gun, sobbing while Joe holds him, and reassures him that everything will be okay. Maybe Joe even buys him breakfast at the pancake house and listens to his story; maybe not.

Here is the best part about spiraling into the Blue Dot of Success and finding your Flow. Joe's new goal is to die in a state of Flow. If the young man pulls the trigger, Joe will succeed in his new goal! His last few minutes on Earth would be filled with love. This is the best part of finding Flow. There is nothing that the gunman can do to prevent Joe from succeeding. Once Joe finds Deep Flow, whatever happens next is perfect! Let go of trying to control the situation and find control of yourself.

Find Deep Flow, and miracles will happen. Joe's assailant dropping the gun and sobbing while Joe comforts him is a miracle. Someone dying while in a Deep Flow state is also a miracle. Joe is in a win/win situation. That is the magic of positive goals and the gift of Flow.

Keith Humphreys, Ph.D., a Stanford psychiatry professor, spent eight years working in hospice. He noted, "One of the most reliable rules was that people die as they had lived. Happy people were happy at the end; crabby people were crabby and anxious people were anxious." If this is the case, perhaps by living in Flow, we increase the chances of passing as we lived, full of grace.

Both Maslow's pyramid and the older chakra model provide us with a beautiful road map for our lives. At birth, we are exclusively focused on meeting the needs of our own personal, immediate survival. As we grow older and those needs are met, we want more personal autonomy, relationships, love. As we pass middle age, our attention will naturally move up to higher chakras.

To age gracefully, we must begin to release attachment to the lower three chakras, which become toxic goals as we approach this journey's conclusion. First, release attachment to external control. You may be asked to give up your car keys, your checkbook, etc. Redirect this third chakra energy into the fifth chakra. Rather than striving to control your environment and those around you, focus on self-control. Learn to control your reaction to the external environment. Next, take the second chakra's energy, the desire for immortality through grandchildren, and redirect that to the sixth chakra, desiring wisdom and finding immortality in your relationship to the infinite. Finally, at the very end, take the energy of the first chakra, immediate personal survival, and redirect that into the seventh chakra, self-transcendence.

Remember, the lower chakras that served you well when you were young become toxic to you in old age and must be released. The choice you face is whether you release attachment to the first three chakras willingly or unwillingly.

Chapter Seven

CLOSING THOUGHTS

"Dreaming is wonderful, goal setting is crucial, but action is supreme. To make something great happen you must get busy and make it happen. Take that action step today that will put you on your path to achievement." ~ Greg Werner

Let your vision be a life lived in Flow. Remember, seeking Flow is not at all the same as avoiding boredom or fear. In each situation and each moment, seek Flow. Not by avoiding boring or scary situations, but instead by using those situations as opportunities to practice controlling your reaction to such environments. When you learn to control your response (by controlling your goals), you convert boring and scary situations into Flow experiences. As you expand your Flow window, you will experience less boredom and fear regardless of your environment, and increasingly, you will discover moments of profoundly satisfying Deep Flow.

Let go of the past, occupy the present, and lean into the future, especially when that future is uncertain.

Cliff Notes

Goals tend to be sticky. Easy to pick up, challenging to set aside. The best time to identify a toxic goal is before you pick it up.

Goals should be

- Authentically yours

- Specific & positive (Blue Dot)

- Challenging but achievable (Flow)

- Set in the future (not status quo)

- Aligned with your Vision and Mission

- Linked to a timeline

- Chosen to inspire commitment

Remember to hold tight to your vision, stay in Flow, and be flexible as you navigate the terrain in between.

The Noble Art of Swallowing Frogs!

If you occasionally suffer from procrastination, as I do, there are hundreds of books that address this dreadful affliction. Here, I will share my favorite procrastination meme. Nicolas Chamfort, a French writer of the 18th century, known for his wit, was the first to advocate swallowing frogs. But Mark Twain is most closely associated with this practice in the U.S. Over time, countless variations on this theme have emerged. Here are three of my favorites:

- Eat a frog first thing in the morning, and the worst of your day is behind you

- If you have to eat a frog, it is best not to spend too much time thinking about it

- If you have to eat two frogs, don't start with the smallest

What Next?

The ideas in this book are worthless to you in theory. It is only in practice that you can master these skills. Right now, everything hangs in the balance! The question of whether or not you just wasted good money to buy this book, and precious time in reading it, will be answered by what you do next. Find your own path forward, in Flow, seeking Deeper Flow. Take your first step on that path before the moment passes you by.

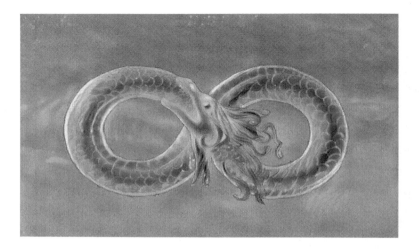

"When I see I am nothing, that is wisdom. When I see I am everything, that is love. My life is a movement between these two."
~ Nisargadatta Maharaj

AFTERWORD

How Can You Help?

If you share our belief that individuals, society, and the world would benefit from more people understanding and applying the principles we have discussed, please take a moment to rate and write a review of this book on Amazon. This is the surest way to raise a book's profile on the platform and help others find it.

Visit toxicgoals.com to access full color illustrations from this book, or to sign up for the author's newsletter and find out about workshops, retreats, and future projects.

You can find out more about Charles's Yoga offerings at his personal website www.yogateacher.com

ACKNOWLEDGMENTS

First and foremost, I need to thank Wilson McVicker for supporting this project over the last eight years. I am also indebted to all of the Yoga Students over 30 years from whom I have learned so much. This book's ideas have been inspired and filtered through countless conversations with these students after class, during workshops, and especially on retreats.

Next, I want to thank Patricia Lewis for setting the stage for me to consider writing a book. English, especially grammar, was my least favorite subject in high school and college. Patricia convinced me to collaborate with her in offering a yoga & writing retreat in 1996. Over the next two decades, we offered 50 or more yoga & writing retreats in the U.S., Mexico, Costa Rica, and Guatemala. This is how I fell in love with writing.

Our Yoga & Writing Retreats follow the Amherst Writers & Artists' (AWA) guidelines, as set forth by the founder, Pat Schneider. This safe and supportive environment allowed novices like myself to sit alongside and benefit from truly gifted and accomplished writers and not feel intimidated. To all of the AWA members, a heartfelt thank you for your work in helping writers find their voice and the courage to share.

Lastly, I need to thank those who played a more direct role in publishing my book. Michelle Fajkus, Ruth Leibowitz, Ph.D., and Giselle Ostman helped edit my manuscript. Gudjon Bergmann of Flaming Leaf Press is my publisher and has offered advice throughout the process. I cannot thank these four enough.

ABOUT THE AUTHOR

Charles MacInerney, E-RYT-500, C-IAYT, is one of the most accomplished yoga teachers in the U.S.

In 2015, he received the Yoga Service Award from the Consul General of India, recognizing his efforts over three decades to help government, universities, businesses, hospitals, and organizations integrate yoga, meditation, and spirituality into the workplace.

Charles started practicing Yoga, Meditation, and Pranayama in 1972 at age eleven and has taught over 20,000 students. He founded the Free-Day-of-Yoga and is a co-founder of both the Texas Yoga Retreat and the Living Yoga Program (one of the most successful yoga teacher training programs in the Southwest with 400 graduates teaching in 45 states and 15 countries).

For the past 25 years, Charles has led yoga & writing retreats throughout the U.S., Costa Rica, Mexico, and Guatemala. He is certified to lead writing groups by the Amherst Writers and Artists (AWA).

Charles is also a professional public speaker. He has taught over 400 workshops on a wide variety of topics, including Goal Setting; Peak Performance; Improving Concentration; Overcoming Anxiety; Creative Solutions for Boredom; Will Power; Balance; Mind-Body Health; Meditation; Breathing; and Yoga.

His clients have included: 3M, IBM, Apple, Sematech, Motorola, several hospitals and universities, including extensive work with The University of Texas (working with faculty, students, the women's athletic program, the departments of architecture, art, music, dance, and kinesiology). He has presented at over 50 regional, national, and international conferences, including a workshop on Mind-Body Creativity at the SXSW Interactive Media Conference, Yoga for Trauma Victims at the International Association of Yoga Therapists' Symposium on Yoga Therapy and Research, and Mind-Body Medicine at the American Medical Student Association's annual conference.

Charles has created and run two hospital based Cardiac Yoga programs.

Visit his personal website at yogateacher.com for more details or to contact him directly.

Made in the USA
Columbia, SC
05 September 2024